TWELVE
LITERARY
WALKS

TWELVE LITERARY WALKS

WITH ORDNANCE SURVEY MAPS

CHRISTOPHER SOMERVILLE

W.H. ALLEN · LONDON

*For George and Ruth, with happy memories of
Dymchurch and Gatehouse-of-Fleet*

Maps copyright © Ordnance Survey 1985

Text copyright © Christopher Somerville 1985

Phototypeset by Sunrise Setting, Devon
Printed and bound in Great Britain by
Mackays of Chatham Ltd, Kent
for the Publishers W.H. Allen & Co. PLC
44 Hill Street, London W1X 8LB

ISBN 0 491 03294 3 (W.H. Allen hardcover edition)
ISBN 0 86379 019 4 (Comet Books softcover edition)

Contents

Foreword

Britain's landscape is rich in literary associations. Whether this is a book for readers who walk a bit, or walkers who read a bit, I leave it to you, dear reader, to decide. Here are twelve authors in their settings, and a walk around each one. The authors vary from the celebrated to the obscure, from the well-loved to the well-nigh forgotten. Their settings range from the tranquillity of Devon to the marshes of Kent, the windy heights of Watership Down to the rolling Welsh borderland, the mountains of the Lake District to the coal-bearing industrial Durham landscape. Most of the books are the mainstay of every library and bookshop; one or two of them have to be hunted for in second-hand bargain boxes and dusty bookcases.

Some of these walks are gentle strolls, others more challenging. Each one is a journey of discovery, whether you are meeting these writers and their countryside for the first time, or returning to them as old friends.

So gird your loins, reader, to walk with a motley crew — otter-hunters, Victorian lovers, rabbits, smugglers, parsons, public-schoolboys, village lads, curates, the daughters of clergymen, poets, pitmen and private detectives!

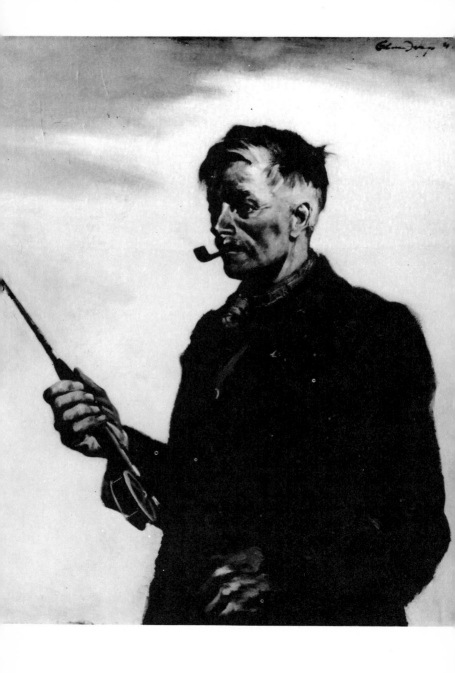

Tarka's Last Hunt

Tarka the Otter by Henry Williamson
First published by Putnam, 1927
Penguin paperback, 1971

(Town Mills — Taddiport Bridge — Rothern Bridge — Furzebeam Hill — Great Torrington — Town Mills. About four miles' easy walk by riverside and hillside paths)

O.S.– 1:50,000 Sheet No. 180 — 'Barnstaple and Ilfracombe'
1:25,000 Sheets No. SS 41/51 'Great Torrington' and SS 42/52 'Bideford'

In 1921 Henry Williamson felt his life had come to a dead end. Already grey-haired at twenty-six, he had been battered into a spiritual and emotional wreck by four years' continuous service in the Great War. That inner scarring was to taint the rest of his life and colour all his subsequent development, both as a man and as a writer.

A brief attachment as a reporter to the *Weekly Sketch* had ended ignominiously when he failed to get an interview with a fashionable nobleman on the subject of 'Will Side Whiskers Return?' Now, rudderless and depressed, ejected from the family home by a father who accused him of writing as an 'excuse to loaf', he shook the dust of all human society from his feet and plunged into North Devon, the land of red deer and red earth, with £5 in his pocket and a desperate need to rebuild a shattered life. Seven years later he was collecting the Hawthornden Prize as author of a best-seller that captivated the entire country — *Tarka the Otter*.

Born of countless hours of sitting and watching the minute operations of nature along the river Torridge, and written agonizingly through seventeen reconstructions while his

Opposite: *Henry Williamson by Edward Seago, courtesy*

new-born baby slept in the crook of his arm, *Tarka* made his name, fame and fortune; but these assets came without the blessing of peace of mind. Other books followed — among them, *Salar the Salmon*, another meticulous and poetic account of a local river and its wildlife, this time the Taw; collections of short stories about village life and nature; later, a four-part compilation of his early novels entitled *The Flax of Dream*; and a saga in fifteen volumes, *A Chronicle of Ancient Sunlight*, whose five books covering the Great War stand comparison with the greatest accounts of that terrible experience.

Henry Williamson's life from *Tarka* onwards, right up until his death on 13th August 1977, was a painful journey through disillusionment and public neglect, relieved from time to time by periods of tranquillity. He had a long flirtation with Fascism, seeing Sir Oswald Mosley and Adolf Hitler as strong leaders dedicated to the restoration of ancient values that Williamson admired in a naïve and credulous way. He was briefly imprisoned as an undesirable at the start of the Second World War, spent the war years building up a farm in Norfolk only to lose it in 1945, remarried in 1949 after his first marriage had disintegrated, and returned to the hut he had built with the money *Tarka* had brought him, at Georgeham, in North Devon. Here he lived until the last few years of his life, slowly finishing *A Chronicle of Ancient Sunlight*, often taking and giving offence in his relationships because of his prickly sensibilities and inward torment.

Yet he was capable of inspiring deep affection, and always had time (and money) for the young and struggling writer. This lonely and much misunderstood man will be remembered and admired, when the dust of his political and personal idiosyncrasies has long settled, for what is probably the finest account ever written of nature closely observed and lovingly recorded — the universally adored *Tarka the Otter*.

Williamson himself had raised an otter cub in his tiny cottage, and had in vain searched the Two Rivers, Taw and Torridge, for months, when it had escaped after an accident with a gin trap. The realism of the book strikes all its readers, for it was written straight from personal experience. Marvellously close observation of plants, water in all its

Town Mills

moods, trees, small riverside mammals, fish and birds packs
every page. Yet the story also spellbinds the reader with high
drama, humour and pathos as Tarka learns the facts of life in
encounters with poachers, salmon, Old Nog the heron and the
fearsome otter-hounds whose leader, the implacable
Deadlock, is a grim Nemesis throughout the story, always at
Tarka's heels and certain one day to come to grips with him in
a final showdown. Many powerful scenes stay imprinted on the
mind: the hunting and killing of Tarka's father; Greymuzzle,
Tarka's mate, sacrificing her life to save him when they are
cornered by a gang of farmhands and their dog; their cub, born
blind in a terrible ice-bound winter in the estuary, freezing to
death along with Marland Jimmy, the deaf old dog-otter from
the clay moors. If Henry Williamson's writing is sentimental,
as some critics have claimed, it is sentiment of a sensitive mind
which did not baulk at recording the red teeth and claws of
nature. Inevitably, though, the most powerful and haunting
part of the book is the last hunt of Tarka, from Town Mills near
the hill-top town of Great Torrington down the river Torridge
to its climax at the river-mouth. Thanks to the wonderful detail
of Henry Williamson's description of the hunt, we can follow
every twist and turn of the chase for most of its course.

* * *

The Wheel, Town Mills

The trail of the last hunt of Tarka the Otter really begins in Darkham Wood, which lies just south of New Bridge and Town Mills Hotel. Through the wood trickles a narrow leat, or artificial water-course, built to provide water for the elm-wood wheels of Town Mills. Here Tarka took refuge when the Master of the otter-hounds in his yellow waistcoat first spotted him in the river and cried the fatal 'Tally-Ho!' that set Deadlock and the otter-hounds on his track.

However, Darkham Woods are in private ownership (though permission to follow the leat through the woods may be sought at Town Mills Hotel), so the walk begins in the grounds of the hotel itself (500184), where the A386 road descends the steep hill from Great Torrington and makes a sharp right-hand bend to cross the Torridge over New Bridge. Since the days when wood was sawn and corn ground at Town Mills, the buildings have been used for various purposes; they were bought in a semi-derelict state a few years ago by Pip and Denis Ives, who have established a hotel famed far and wide among fishermen. Just behind the castellated ramparts of the square, solid hotel are the original stone mill buildings, where water from the now sluggish and overgrown leat still turns a great spoked water-wheel. They were grinding corn on the afternoon that Tarka swam out of the leat. After a shout of 'One o'clock!' had caused the wheel to slow down and stop, the otter climbed up the slippery wooden slats of the wheel to squat in the topmost trough while Deadlock bayed in frustration against the grating below. For a silent hour Tarka stayed hidden there while the hounds cast around for his scent. Then the workmen's dinner-hour was over, the wheel began to revolve again, the otter was thrown down into the stream that flowed from the wheel to the river, and the last hunt was on.

Ten yards downstream from New Bridge on the right-hand bank of the Torridge, a walled lane leads down to a wide, muddy path above the river. This is the dried-up bed of a disused canal, a continuation of the Darkham Woods leat, that once carried the produce of Town Mills downriver to Bideford and the sea. High up on the steep hill to the right stands Great Torrington, called the 'Town on the Hill' by Henry

Williamson, and on the left, across the river, neatly hedged and rounded farmland rolls to the skyline. The obelisk that can be seen standing out against the sky above the old canal bears an interesting inscription which will be studied on the return journey! Woodpeckers call among the sycamores, birch and ash trees which line the river-bank, while the neat tracks of animals and the muddier ones of fishermen descend the slope from canal-bed to bank, fringed with celandines and hart's-tongue ferns. Looking back upriver you can see the arches of New Bridge above which Tarka hid before braving the barrier of poles with which the huntsmen stirred the water into a frightening mass of bubbles as they stood knee-deep across the river. Once past the legs of the men in the water, he had a long straight stretch of water to swim, surfacing to breathe at either bank in turn, before darting on underwater as the hounds plunged through the shallows or swam downstream after him. The path along the old canal-bed continues, shaded by trees, towards Taddiport Bridge (487187); but just under the castle battlements high above on the hill, a scramble down the bank leads to a riverside path which can be followed between clumps of wild garlic to an area of tussocky ground where kingcups, docks and wild daffodils grow among the brambles. Here Tarka left the water to run among balsam stems which were crushed by the feet of the hounds on his trail. Soon he was in the water again and swimming under one of the three arches of ancient Taddiport Bridge, which connects the little settlement of Taddiport, in the Middle Ages a leper colony, with the houses of Mill Street, rising up the hill towards the town in a stepped rank.

Now the scene is dominated by the smoking chimneys of Torrington Creamery, whose curved 1930s walls stand on the bank above the river. From Taddiport Bridge the riverside path can be followed down a deeply rutted lane which brings you out above a weir built recently for the Creamery's use. Between Taddiport Bridge and the weir lies Williamson's 'ridge of shillets, long and wide as the broken hull of a sailing ship'. These are two islets of stone in midstream, where Tarka landed to try to hide his scent in the long grass.

Below the weir, Servis Wood hangs darkly above the left-hand bank of the river, overlooking a strong-smelling

Taddiport Bridge seen from the Creamery weir

sewage works, where the official right of way is broken.
Retrace your steps to Taddiport Bridge and walk uphill to the
Torridge Inn at the corner of Mill Street — bar snacks and real
ale can be sampled here. A right of way passes from the old
canal path across the main road and right through the busy
complex of the Creamery, where milk tankers are constantly
arriving and departing. A better option is to mount the steps in
front of the Torridge Inn and climb the steep pavement up Mill
Street to a little walled alley between numbers 86 and 84, which
runs out onto the open common land above the terrace. The
path goes over the first crossways and turns downhill to the left
at a bench inscribed *'Presented by F. Edwards. Sept. 1954'*,
from which there is a splendid view over the Creamery and
Servis Wood to the tower of Monkleigh Church on its distant
hillside. After crossing the B3227 road, a muddy track
descends to join the old canal-bed again, now a tarred road, by
the gates of the sewage works (483192).

The path runs north-north-east above the Torridge, with a
view of Service Farm and Drummet's Mill on the opposite side
of the river. The slanted blocks of an old gorse-grown quarry
are piled on the right of the path, which soon passes under an
iron bridge carrying the disused railway from the clay pits at
Meeth to nearby Torrington station and on to Bideford and

Barnstaple. This bridge is an extension of a long black girder viaduct on square stone piers, which brings the railway across the river. Just before the viaduct a brook winds away southwards from the left bank of the river (481195); up this stream Tarka travelled with his mother and two sisters when he was still a cub, following the twisting water-course through Pencleave Woods and Vinney Copse before seeking other brooks that led the otters up to Merton Moors. Here they played with Marland Jimmy, the old otter who lived in the string of ponds developed from pits hollowed out by the clay-diggers that still work today in those bleak uplands.

Passing under the railway bridge in his last swim for life, Tarka came to Elm Island (480197). This boat-shaped hummock in the river just upstream from Rolle Bridge is in fact an extension of the right bank of the Torridge at most seasons of the year, the right-hand channel between bank and island being dry and colonized by land plants — Williamson named them as 'hawkweed, ragwort and St John's Wort', and 'the broad leaves and white flowers of wild garlic growing under the trees'. You can look down on Elm Island from the old canal-bed path, which climbs up to Rolle Bridge and which, on the day of the hunt, was full of cars whose occupants had come to view the kill. They saw nothing of Tarka, who lay flat among the stinking garlic plants while Deadlock sniffed in vain for his elusive scent. It was the kennel-boy who spotted him, and in the shock of the moment dropped the chain which restrained the two terriers, Bite'm and Biff, who were brought along to push otters out of narrow hiding-places which the sturdier hounds could not reach. Tarka fought desperately with the terriers and managed to roll over the edge of Elm Island and into the river for a few more precious hours of life.

Henry Williamson does not mention Rolle Bridge, which was built just after *Tarka the Otter* was published in 1927 to take the increasing volume of motor traffic that was threatening to shake to pieces the narrow and beautiful old Rothern Bridge (478197), a few yards downstream. Williamson, with his unerring eye for the interaction of nature and man-made structures, did note that Rothern Bridge's 'three stone arches, bearing heavy motor-transport beyond their old age, showed the cracks of suffering that the ferns were filling green'. Looking down from Rolle Bridge, the older structure has regained its dignity in retirement; only the cars of fishermen pass across it today, and it may well outlive its overshadowing younger brother.

Where Rolle Bridge now stands stood the Master of the Hunt on the bank, watching Tarka inching his way smoothly downstream on the river-bed. Below Rothern Bridge another line of men stretched across the river, stirring up the water with their poles; but Tarka braved the hazard, passed the dippers and wagtails on the shillets beyond, and swam on towards his fate. From this point the land beside the river is in private ownership, and to get a proper sight of the next stages of the hunt you should cross the A386 road above Rothern Bridge where it passes over the station bridge and the grassy platforms and rusty rails below. The station buildings of orange and grey stone still stand, boarded up and empty; the stationmaster's garden is still tended by some loving hand, and the Victorian letterbox in the door is still used.

Just beyond the railway bridge a gateway leads onto Great Torrington Common, where a zig-zag path mounts up Furzebeam Hill to the golf course at the top. It is a hard climb, but from the seat at the north-western end of the summit a marvellous panorama is laid out at your feet. The Torridge snakes in a great S-bend round Beam Mansion (473207), bisected by the slightly curving railway line that crosses the river on three girder bridges, two of which are seen from the hill. The long sparkling bar of Beam Weir leans across the river just below the little bridge, its rushing sound clearly audible, and the white walls and flashing windows of Beam Mansion (now Beam College, a special school) are cradled in the elbow of the ox-bow among trees. Flat green cow-pasture lies to left and right of the river, while behind Beam Mansion rear the crags and scars of quarries against a wonderful backdrop of round wooded hills. This kind of view, natural to the West Country and stunning in any weather conditions, makes the uphill climber thankful that he has to stop and get his breath back — for it certainly takes the breath away all over again!

From this vantage point the next act of the drama can be followed without stirring from your seat. Tarka reached Beam Pool above the weir, and climbed up onto the roots of a sycamore tree to rest and hide from the relentless hounds, still hot on his track. The scent led them to the sycamore tree — and to fresh sport. The cub Tarquol, Tarka's son by his mate White-tip, was resting there when Tarka appeared; but, unlike his parent, the cub could not endure the snuffling of the hounds at the entrance to the hiding-place, the yapping of Bite'm and Biff, and the terrible thumping of an iron bar above his head. Soon he was in the river and up the bank, running a losing race across the meadows and round Furzebeam Hill before the final moments in the thorn hedge by the railway line.

'Tarquol ran out of the thorns just before Render's muzzle pushed into his hiding-place; but hounds leapt the low hedge and overtook him, before he had gone very far on his short, tired legs. Deadlock seized him and shook him and threw him into the air. Tarquol sprang up as soon as he fell, snapping and writhing as more jaws bit onto his body, crushed his head, cracked his ribs, his paws and his rudder. Among the brilliant hawkbits — little sunflowers of the meadow — he was picked up and dropped again, trodden on and wrenched and broken, while the screaming cheers and whoops of sportsmen mingled with the growling rumble of hounds at worry. Tarquol fought them until he was blinded, and his jaws were smashed. He had gone home before Tarka.'

Meanwhile Tarka, unaware of the fate he had brought on his offspring, swam down to the weir and climbed up to a resting-place on the sill. Here he might have stayed safely; but the old poacher, Shiner, who had lost a finger-joint during a close encounter with Tarka and his mother, spotted him from the railway bridge, and the chase was on again. Shiner, by the way, appears in more angelic form in Henry Williamson's other full-length book about the country of the Two Rivers, *Salar the Salmon*, in which he has given up his poaching and turned to conservation — a forerunner of some modern nature-lovers! — though not yet reconciled to 'they bliddy baillies', the water-bailiffs who are still the bane of night-walkers with long nets in this part of the world. Shiner, an old-time poacher whose only aim was a salmon for his tea, would hardly recognize his modern brothers-in-crime, well-organized gangs equipped with sophisticated poisons and fast cars who poach for the freezers of city-dwellers, and against whom the present-day bailiffs employ infra-red night-sight devices.

Back and forth went Tarka, now in the water meadows, now in the river, under Canal Bridge (473209), which once carried the old canal over the Torridge a few yards upstream of the third railway bridge, and on to Leaning Willow Island (478216), an aptly named islet in midstream between Beam and the village of Weare Giffard. Each time the hounds closed with him, he twisted and snapped himself free, his vision blurring and his body reaching the last stages of exhaustion. Lines of men and women in their bright uniforms prodded the river-bed with sticks, often seeing the otter as he rose to vent, too tired to look for a place to hide in the banks. During the sixth hour of the chase he disappeared and again the entire hunt was baffled; only one girl heard and saw him sneeze away a dragonfly which had settled on his nostrils as he lay concealed by a fallen willow branch, and she stayed fearfully quiet until a second sneeze alerted her nearby father – 'Tally-Ho!'

Tossed and bitten many times and weary to death, Tarka still fought on, wriggling away from a huntsman's iron-pointed pole which had pinned him to a shillet bank. But at long last his approaching death moved him by instinct to one final effort to reach the sea. Near the mouth of the river, he met and closed with the leading hound, Deadlock, for the last time, pulled him down and drowned him. While the hunters were standing round the body of the hound, Tarka drifted with the tide past Bideford and Appledore where Torridge meets Taw, and out to sea.

'And while they stood there silently, a great bubble rose out of the depths and broke, and as they watched, another bubble shook the surface, and broke; and there was a third bubble in the sea-going waters, and nothing more.'

The return to Town Mills is made by way of the splendid high-level footpath along Great Torrington Common, which starts opposite the railway station (481197). The narrow tarmac path runs below the A386 road on a terrace high above the river, which is seen below in occasional glimpses between the tree-tops. There are several benches along the way which give an excellent view of the course of the Torridge as it skirts the foot of the hill, with Cross House standing bravely out in its collar of trees on North Hill on the other side of the valley. After crossing a common of gorse bushes and bracken, followed by the B3227 road, bear left onto the higher of two paths (485192) which hugs the garden walls of houses, looking down to the steaming Creamery by Taddiport Bridge, a busy industrial reference point in peerless surroundings. By a tall and shapely ilex tree you descend Warren Lane, turning uphill at its junction with Mill Street to join South Street, the main artery of Great Torrington. After a couple of hundred yards, turn right into the car park and make for the south-eastern corner. A plain stone gateway leads out onto Castle Hill and the second of two heart-stopping views on this walk (495189). Quite without warning the ground plunges away nearly three hundred feet to the winding Torridge, producing a feeling of having just walked off the edge of a cliff. At your back are the walls of the castle, built about the turn of the thirteenth century by the de Toriton family. Unfortunately they omitted to obtain the necessary royal permission to build their castle, and had it demolished by the Sheriff of Devon in 1228. It was rebuilt in 1338–9. At your feet is the dramatic escarpment, and in front of you mile upon mile of wooded hills, folding upon each other up to the skyline.

Turn left onto a path which snakes downhill towards Town Mills Hotel and New Bridge, set with the harmony of a painting against the dark waves of Torrington Wood. On the way down, the path passes the monument, seen outlined from below earlier in the walk. Its quaint and enthusiastic inscription reads: *Erected June 1818 to commemorate the Battle of Waterloo June 1815. Peace to the souls of the HEROES*!!!' This modest and slightly mis-shapen needle of stone that has weathered nearly two hundred years of Devon winds and rains was presented by the ladies of the town.

From the obelisk the track continues steeply downhill to a brook and follows it down to the old canal-bed. Here you turn left and make your way back to the road, the arches of New Bridge, and the ever-revolving water-wheel behind Town Mills Hotel where Tarka the Otter squatted in the shadows and waited for Deadlock and death. May his descendants, now precariously re-established in the Torridge, continue to increase and flourish.

The Henry Williamson Society
c/o The Membership Secretary, Longclose, Langtree, Torrington, Devon EX38 8NR
Formed in 1980 '. . . to encourage by all appropriate means, a wider readership and deeper understanding of the literary heritage left to us by the major twentieth-century writer, Henry Williamson.'
The Society meets regularly.

The Otter Haven Project
Launched in 1977 by the Vincent Wildlife Trust and the Fauna Preservation Society to establish and protect suitable areas for the introduction and safeguarding of otters in the wild.
For information contact Elizabeth Lenton (Regional Co-ordinator — South West, Wessex & Southern Water Authority Areas), 5 St Stephen's Court, Bath, Avon BA1 5PG.

Town Mills Hotel
c/o Pip and Denis Ives, Town Mills Hotel, Torrington, Devon EX38 8PH (Tel: Torrington (08052) 2114)

Local Library
North Devon Area Library, Vicarage Street, Barnstaple EX32 7EJ

Useful books
Henry Williamson — the Man, the Writings (a symposium of essays by friends and acquaintances of Henry Williamson). Published by Tabb House, Padstow, Cornwall, 1980

Henry by Daniel Farson. Published by Michael Joseph, 1982

Through the Undercliff with the French Lieutenant's Woman

The French Lieutenant's Woman by John Fowles
First published by Jonathan Cape, 1969
Panther paperback, 1971

(The Cobb, Lyme Regis — Underhill Farm — the Undercliff — Axmouth. A strenuous seven miles by steep, narrow and slippery paths through overgrown woodland, with no accessible escape routes. Proper walking clothes and footwear essential. Return journey from Axmouth to Lyme Regis should be arranged in advance.)

O.S.– 1:50,000 Sheet No. 193 'Taunton and Lyme Regis'
1:25,000 Sheet No. SY 29/39 'Lyme Regis and Axminster'

One windy evening in November 1814, a merry party of seven young people are taking a seaside stroll. They are walking on the top of a rough stone jetty that curves out into the choppy waters of a cliff-encircled bay. The young ladies clutch at their companions for support as the strong sea-wind buffets them, and soon one of the gentlemen suggests that they descend to a lower level where they will be sheltered from the gale. The party pick their way carefully down a flight of crude steps; but the last young lady, half excited and half teasing, begs her companion to jump her down. The sensation of flying into a strong man's arms is so delightful that she runs up the steps again for a second jump. But the gentleman is not quite ready, she is half a second too early, and plunges through his arms to knock herself unconscious on the lower pavement.

Consternation!

Opposite: *John Fowles*

One equally windy day nearly 170 years later, the cloaked figure of a woman stands at the end of the same stone jetty. Her back is to the film cameras, but from the whipping of the heavy black material around her body one can tell that she is tall and graceful. The onlookers admire the fortitude of the actress as she stands unmoving, drenched with green spray that bursts over the jetty wall, a lonely and enigmatic shape.

Suddenly the wind whisks the hood back from her face, exposing not the classic cheek-bones and Titian locks of the beautiful Meryl Streep, but the bristling jaw of the man standing in for her, roped down against the gale and cursing through chattering teeth.

Cut!

The setting for both these scenes (Louisa Musgrove's fall in Jane Austen's *Persuasion* and Sarah Woodruff's seaward gazing in the film version of John Fowles's *The French Lieutenant's Woman*) is the Cobb, an ancient breakwater that juts into Lyme Bay from the western end of the little Dorset seaside town of Lyme Regis. Lyme's history is a long and chequered affair. By 1284, the year of its Royal Charter, it was already a thriving port trading across the Channel; by the time of Queen Elizabeth 1, goods were leaving the Cobb for destinations beyond the Mediterranean and the Atlantic. Fine houses were built in Lyme, and its merchants grew fat on the profitable foreign trade.

By 1750 the town was virtually dead as a trading centre, strangled by its inadequate approach roads and shallow harbour — wheeled traffic could not enter the town, and ships drawing more than a few feet could not reach the Cobb. Then came the seaside resort boom of the late eighteenth-century and a resurgence of Lyme's fortunes. New houses were built on the hills behind the town, and service industries for the holiday trade replaced salt- and cloth-making, shipping and fishing. Today only a handful of boats go out from Lyme.

The townsfolk are noted for their independence of mind and their close-knit self-reliance. During the seventeenth century they backed one winner — Parliament, through an epic two-month siege; and one loser — the Duke of Monmouth landed at Lyme on his way to Sedgemoor and an ignominious death for himself and thousands of his followers. The Fane family ran the town as a pocket borough for a hundred years, returning two Members of Parliament right up to 1832 and the Reform Act.

Lyme's main claim to fame, however, is based on events that took place long before recorded history. Mary Anning, born in 1799, became a celebrity at the age of eleven when she helped to discover the fossilized skeleton of an Ichthyosaurus or Fish Lizard in the cliffs between Lyme and Charmouth; and countless palaeontologists, professional and amateur, have followed in her footsteps. Lyme's position in the middle of a massive band of grey Jurassic shales and limestone, about 150 million years old and known as Blue Lias, makes it a unique paradise for fossil-hunters. Here are whorl-shaped ammonites, nautilus shells and bullet-like belemnites by the plastic bag-full, and, more rarely, spidery echinoderms, crinoids or sea-lilies, bony fish, coprolites (dinosaur droppings, which when split and polished show a delicate inner pattern) — as well as the Ichthyosaurus and another monster, the Plesiosaurus, which grew up to 20 feet long and might be a close cousin of the Loch Ness monster. Although the Lyme cliffs are extremely dangerous to climb, being crumbly and unstable, rain and tides obligingly wash out these and many other fossils, some to be picked up by any casual beach-stroller, others to be detected only by expert eyes. The Fossil Shop in Bridge Street contains a large selection of this unearthed treasure, most of it for sale.

There are more specimens on show in the Lyme Regis Museum, just across the road from the Fossil Shop. Though small, the museum is a gem, built around a winding staircase, and repays a second and third visit, like many of the nooks and crannies in Lyme. An excellent booklet guide to the area, *Lyme Regis Walkabout*, shows the reader around the town on a series of short walks, and lets him rub shoulders with the famous figures that elbow each other in the tightly packed corridor of Lyme's history — Henry Fielding, trying unsuccessfully to abduct a local heiress on her way to church; anthological Sir Francis Palgrave and antiseptic Lord Lister; the Princess Victoria, and later her wayward son Prince Edward; G.K. Chesterton and Whistler; Beatrix Potter and

Little Pig Robinson. John Fowles himself has written a walker's guide to the town, *Three Town Walks*, in his capacity as Curator of the Lyme Regis Museum.

When Jane Austen stayed at Lyme with her convalescent mother in 1804 (probably at Pyne House in Broad Street), she found it charming, though over-provincial. Fourteen years later the story of Anne Elliot and her lost-and-found-again suitor Captain Wentworth firmly established Lyme in the affections of the reading public. Though the dramatic unmasking of Anne's pursuer, Mr Walter Elliot, takes place at Bath, admirers of *Persuasion* have always been drawn to the traditional scene of Louisa Musgrove's famous fall — the jutting stone treads known as Granny's Teeth set into the wall of the Cobb.

This fossil-studded stone pincer has been well described as an 'arm held before the face of Lyme to protect it from the south-west wind'. Destroyed in a great storm in 1377, the Cobb has been breached at intervals down the years, the last major disaster being in 1824. The events of that traumatic night were recorded in eye-witness paintings that hang in the Lyme Regis Museum. During the Middle Ages the collected dues never paid for the upkeep of the Cobb, so the 'Cobb Ale' was introduced. This was a feast (to last not more than twenty days!) attended by rich local worthies, who then contributed to a collection. The accounts for 1601 show an outlay of £34, which covered among other items 4 bottles of wine, $4\frac{1}{2}$cwt of venison, 88 bushels of malt, 25lb of butter, shrimps, capons, cakes and candles. A good time was had by all, and they made £22 profit.

Walking along the unguarded and sloping upper level of the Cobb can be a slippery and frightening business in high wind and spray. Rough stone steps — Granny's Teeth being the most uneven — lead down to the more sheltered lower level, past the dark buildings with their nineteenth-century tariff board and marine aquarium, and out to the jumble of rocks at the end of the Cobb, where the spray cannons with a smack and boom.

Jane Austen was not the only writer to be drawn to the Cobb. John Fowles — sometime public-school head-boy, marine, Oxford graduate and teacher — was haunted by the image of a solitary woman staring out to sea from the historic jetty's seaward end. This seed germinated at length into his celebrated novel *The French Lieutenant's Woman*, to which the hotels and souvenir shops of Lyme already owe a sizeable debt. Since the film of the book was shot in the town, admirers have come each year to see for themselves the steep streets and fossil-laden cliffs, and especially the Cobb where Meryl Streep's stand-in had his soaking.

The French Lieutenant's Woman weaves a subtle and magical spell, constantly setting the reader back on his heels with confrontations and challenges. A complex modern masterpiece of a wolf in Victorian romantic sheep's clothing, it brings past and present face to face. At the opening of the book, its hero, Charles Smithson, is a quizzical, sceptical Darwinist, a Victorian gentleman of leisure whose fossil-hunting and leisurely courtship of his fiancée, Ernestina, leaves him plenty of time to question all the Victorian assumptions — but not actually to defy them. His developing relationship with Sarah Woodruff eventually leads to the breaking off of his engagement and of all his links with the conventional morality of his age. Sarah's wicked past turns out to be a fiction, but he cannot help reaching for the hand she holds out to pull him out of his Victorian self-assurance into the doubts and questionings of the modern world. Bourgeois, respectable Lyme and its inhabitants do not know what to make of the 'scarlet woman', but Charles does. Painfully and hesitantly he kicks off the security blanket, 'a man struggling to overcome history', until at the end of the book he stands beside her, an outcast to his contemporaries who has claimed the right to think and act for himself. At least, that is one of the endings that Fowles offers — there are others, so that the reader has to make up his own mind as to what becomes of Charles. The whole book is shot through with intrusions and asides from the narrator, comparisons between Victorian and present-day perceptions, fingers pointing the reader down side-tracks and up blind alleys.

Standing at the seaward end of the Cobb before starting on the track of Charles and Sarah, you can see the tightly packed pink, white and yellow houses of Lyme rising up the hill away to the right from the beach. It is easy to understand how Lyme has been so isolated in the past, and why it has developed such a strong individual flavour, unlike any other town on the south coast. Hemming it in on both sides are the black and gold cliffs where the fossils lie, stretching away in folded undulations which effectively sealed off the town until they were conquered by the internal combustion engine. All Lyme's external influences came by sea to the Cobb before reaching the town itself.

The cliffs look solid enough — Black Ven, Stonebarrow and Golden Cap to the right, Ware Cleeves to the left — but in fact they are slipping into the sea faster than any other stretch of coastline in England. The rain water seeps down through their top layers of chalk and Upper Greensand, which from the Cobb can be seen exposed in both directions, until it meets a thin band of Gault, a slippery, greasy, impermeable black clay which lies on top of the lower formations of Blue Lias, Rhaetic White Lias and Keuper Marls. These are tilted seawards at an angle of about 5°. The chalk and greensand, lubricated by the rain-sodden Gault, skid down the slope towards the beach, fairly gently as a rule but very occasionally with tremendous violence, displacing a staggering amount of ground. During the walk you can see the result of the greatest of these slips.

On the 29th March 1867 Charles Smithson wandered off along the beach under Ware Cleeves in search of fossils, and climbed blithely up the cliffs of Pinhay Bay into that unique nature reserve, the Undercliff. Nowadays such a beach walk is possible only at extreme low tide; such a climb is completely out of the question because of the unstable nature of the cliffs, which still maroon importunate scramblers every year who have to be taken off to safety by boat or helicopter, and who merit a good tongue-lashing from their rescuers. Our path runs straight up the hillside ahead and along the cliff-tops for six or seven miles in one of the most extraordinary environments in Britain.

*   *   *

22

You begin the walk by heading back along the Cobb to the Shell Shop opposite the harbourmaster's office, then turning west down Ozone Terrace. Just above the Lyme Regis Bowling Club a steep flight of steps winds up the cliff face between bracken, brambles and blackthorn (337917). A stream rustles downhill to the left of the steps in a ferny gully. At the top are a wooden stile and a fingerpost marked *'Coast Path. Seaton 7 m.'* From here on the fingerposts mysteriously telescope the distance to five and a half miles. The well-trodden path, marked with yellow arrows and black acorn symbols, bears left under a wide green valley crowned with the houses of the hamlet of Ware. It goes through two kissing-gates over fields rutted by the ever-widening cracks that are evidence of the constant slipping of the land. From here there are fine views over the Cobb and distant cliffs.

At an ancient crab-apple tree, its twisted branches adorned with lichen, the path crosses the county boundary from Dorset into Devon, and climbs up to a tarmac road by a bungalow (331917). From this point it is a five-minute walk westward to the entrance to the Undercliff Nature Reserve; but before embarking on those five miles of untouched natural woodland, spare a glance down the slope to the left. Half-hidden in trees are the white walls and corrugated roof of Underhill Farm (327915), where John Fowles lived while he was writing *The French Lieutenant's Woman*. The slipping land that underlies the building has torn gaping cracks in the flint garden walls, twisted the slate-roofed shed like a broken-backed animal, and shaken the foundations of the house itself. The neat terraced garden is sadly overgrown, and there are settlement cracks in the window of the conservatory where Meryl Streep and Jeremy Irons rehearsed their play within a play within the film of the book. Of the dairy shed featured in the film, however, there is no trace, as it was specially built for the film and demolished afterwards.

From this spot Fowles was only a short stroll away from a wonderful view over the Cobb and the golden cliffs to the east as far as Chesil Bank and Portland Bill. All is peace, silence and seclusion here: so much so that he began to miss the sounds of passing voices and traffic that kept him in touch with the outside world. A severe land slip that cost the farm one of its fields and threatened the lane caused him to move to the house in Lyme Regis where he still lives.

For centuries the local name for Underhill Farm was the Dairy, and it features in the book under this name. Here Charles stopped for a mug of milk on his way back to Lyme after the first meeting with Sarah in the Undercliff that sent him up the stony path to emancipation. The Undercliff itself, a belt of tangled woodland that straggles along the broken cliff-tops, was declared a National Nature Reserve in 1955 in recognition of its exceptional characteristics. Because of the constant slipping of the land there are no houses or other human intrusions — simply five miles of trees, birds, animals and plants co-existing in splendid isolation.

The notice at the entrance to the reserve above Underhill Farm gives a necessary warning of the difficulties of the path through the Undercliff, which offers at least three hours of strenuous walking on land that is under constant threat of subsidence. Do prepare yourself for a muddy, slippery and undulating track. Adequate walking clothing and a strong pair of legs are of the essence. There are no escape routes or short cuts back to Lyme from the path; the only alternatives are forward to Axmouth or back the way you came. At the far end of the walk, public transport back to Lyme is scanty — there is now no railway, and buses are few and far between. Those without obliging chauffeurs are well advised to arrange to be met by a taxi at Seaton or Axmouth.

Once among the creeper-tangled trees you are walking in the opposite direction to Charles' return journeys to Lyme from his assignations with Sarah, though he probably slipped and scrambled along paths nearer the cliff edge which are now too dangerous to follow. (Serious botanists and naturalists can obtain permission to leave the official path — and essential advice about dangerous locations — if they apply in writing to the Regional Officer, The Nature Conservancy Council, Roughmoor, Bishop's Hull, Taunton TA1 5AA, Somerset). Ours is a muddy trail of boot-marks and splashy hollows, climbing up and down the ridges of past landslips by way of wooden steps and helpful tree roots, dodging in and out of glades where the sun strikes down through the leaves overhead. Tempting side-paths are blocked off by bundles of

A hailstorm out at sea — a view from the Undercliff

branches placed at their mouths to deter walkers from the fissure-ridden interior of the Undercliff. Soon the ear becomes attuned to sounds that accompany the walk throughout its length — the rustle of leaves, trickling of small streams and waterfalls, the far-off crash of waves on the beach below the cliffs, and the ever-present bird song. One hundred and thirty species have been recorded in the reserve. Chiff-chaffs and woodpeckers are frequently heard, and tree-creepers sometimes seen clinging to ivy-strangled trunks. Fallen trees lean and lie everywhere, their rotten carcasses supporting colonies of mosses, ferns and fungi. To the right of the path the inland cliffs rear up above the trees, the white chalk and golden clay of their faces showing where great chunks of land have fallen away in a sliding curve, coming to rest in heaped mounds covered with dense green vegetation. There are occasional glimpses of the sea between the trees to the left, but the attention is concentrated on the luxuriant growth on every side and the wildlife it supports.

25

The path crosses the ruins of old flint walls, witnesses to a celebrated dispute. In the 1840s the ancient right of way through the Undercliff was closed by the owner of Pinhay, John Ames, who established an arboretum here — many of the rare trees still remain. The resultant chain of court actions ended in the House of Lords, where Ames lost his case. Smarting in defeat, he retaliated by walling off the path in long flint corridors, most of which lie off the present path; he also erected narrow stiles that made it hard for crinolined ladies to pass.

The miles are measured off by fingerposts, the only yardsticks of time and distance in this wilderness. About two-thirds of a mile from the entrance the original path was broken by a slip in 1968, and the present track is a diversion inland. It climbs to a stunted thorn tree on the left, whose horizontally growing branch forms a perfect natural seat for a view over the sea. In such a spot Sarah Woodruff perched herself while the fascinated Charles stood by to hear her tale of a glad surrender to the gallant French lieutenant in a boarding-house bed at Weymouth. This story, which Sarah later admitted to having made up, proved an accurate forecast of the scene she and Charles were to play out in mingled joy and horror.

Where the track joins a rough tarred road from Pinhay (317908), the path by which Charles climbed into the Undercliff from his fossil-hunting expedition plunges away on the left to the stony shore at Pinhay Bay. The descent is barred by a red danger warning on a concrete block, itself slewed at an angle by the movement of the ground; but the stream where he was searching for tests (fossil sea-urchins) when he came upon the sleeping Sarah can be heard chuckling in the undergrowth. To the right soars up a three-hundred-foot chalk cliff, brilliantly white beneath the overhanging mats of ivy. The tarmac road slopes steeply downhill between privet bushes and towering ilex trees, their rough bark cracked into small squares like crocodile skin. Soon a low hum is heard from the corrugated-iron water-pumping station between Pinhay Bay and Humble Point (312904). From here there is a view down to the shore, but the old path that once led downwards is now unsafe. This is a convenient boundary to the territory described in *The French Lieutenant's Woman*, and a good place to rest and enjoy the peaceful scene before retracing your steps with Charles to the Dairy and Lyme Regis.

For those with willing hearts and legs, the way lies upwards from the pumping station for the remaining three and a half miles to Axmouth. The new plastic and older iron water-pipes fed by the pumping station snake beside the path as it climbs uphill and forks left by a large and beautiful ilex tree, beyond which lie the ivy-smothered ruins of a cottage, still sheltered by a tattered belt of tall conifers. In narrow crevices in the inland cliffs roost the seagulls, head to wind. Violets, wild iris and the long leaves of wood spurge grow beside the path which mounts to a wooden seat with a fine sea-view (298902). On the cliff edge inland Allhallows School overlooks the Undercliff from a dark mass of trees. Boys from the school have long enjoyed the privilege of private tracks down to the shallows and fossils of Charton Bay, and their surveys in the Undercliff form the basis of much of present-day knowledge about the flora and fauna of the reserve. A major slip a few years ago deprived them of their favourite path to the shore, though the bolder spirits continued to go down by means of Tarzan ropes!

Our path plunges down by steep steps to a hard-surfaced road that passes the foundations of an old water pumping station at the half-way point in the Undercliff walk — two and a half miles from both Lyme and Seaton, according to the fingerpost. Flourishing bushes each side show the influence of Sir William Peek, the builder of the mansion that now houses Allhallows School — box, privet, yew, rhododendron and evergreen oak, as well as sweet chestnut and a variety of firs. As the chalk in the soil comes nearer to the surface, the path becomes progressively stickier and more slippery. Many kinds of spongy lichens and mosses suck up nourishment from water-logged tree trunks lying among the mats of undergrowth.

Nearing the end of the reserve, the trees begin to thin out as the path crosses the outskirts of an ash wood (281895). This is no ordinary wood, but the only recorded example this century of a naturally developing ash wood, and it stands in the shadow of the greatest landslip ever documented on this coast. On Christmas Eve, 1839, an estimated eight million tons of land, measuring about twenty acres in all, sank away from its anchoring cliff between Dowlands and Bindon, forming an enormous chasm nearly two hundred feet deep, half a mile long and four hundred feet wide. As it slid and tilted down and inwards, the huge mass of intact land kicked up and outwards with its seaward foot, raising a reef three-quarters of a mile long and forty feet high about one hundred yards from the shore. Storms soon washed away the reef, but the great slab of displaced ground remained slanted across the chasm, much of it so little disturbed during the slip that crops growing on the top were harvested the following year. The Lyme Regis Museum has a contemporary coloured print of the event with Union Jacks, gaitered and bonneted sightseers, and carousing harvesters beneath the raw new cliffs of the Chasm. The slab of land isolated in the Chasm, some fifteen acres known as Goat Island, supports a closed chalk grassland community, unaffected by, and developing differently from, the surrounding land. Brambles are making inroads into the grass on Goat Island, and from the path it is hard to identify its exact shape and position (275895), so overgrown are both the Island and the Chasm.

The end of the Undercliff reserve is heralded by views far and wide over Seaton and the coastline beyond. Trees and bird-song are left behind as the path winds between impenetrable scrub before a final short, steep haul up wooden steps to a stile (271895). From here a signposted path crosses cliff-top fields to a narrow lane (263902), where you make your choice between turning left and dropping down over the golf course to Axmouth Bridge and Seaton, or continuing on over another two fields to the steep lane into Axmouth. The only strenuous task still ahead is brushing the mud from your boots – or entire person if it has been raining — before the return journey to Lyme.

Although half the walk has been outside the province of *The French Lieutenant's Woman*, you will end up most fittingly at your starting-point — the spray-spattered, squat old Cobb where Charles Smithson received a death-wound on behalf of the whole Victorian age when he first looked into the eyes of Sarah Woodruff.

The Lyme Regis Museum
Bridge Street, Lyme Regis, Dorset DT7 3QA

The Lyme Regis Society
c/o The Lyme Regis Museum
The Society holds regular meetings, and is dedicated to local history.

Information on the Undercliff
The Heritage Coast Officer. Tel: Lyme Regis (029 74) 5226

Local Library
Dorchester Library, Colliton Park, Dorchester, Dorset DT1 1XJ

Useful books
(All these are obtainable from the Museum or from Serendip Books, 11, Broad Street, Lyme Regis)
Lyme Regis — Three Town Walks by John Fowles. Published by the Friends of the Lyme Regis Museum, 1983
A Brief History of Lyme by John Fowles. Published by the Friends of the Lyme Regis Museum, 1981
Landslips near Lyme Regis by Muriel A. Arber (reprinted from the Proceedings of the Geologists' Association, Vol. 84, Part 2 (1973), pp. 121–133). Published by Serendip Books, Lyme Regis, 1976
The Axmouth/Lyme Regis Undercliffs National Nature Reserve by T.J. Wallace. Published by Serendip Books, Lyme Regis, 1976
The Seaton to Lyme Regis Coast Walk by Norman Barry. Published 1982
Lyme Bay Fossils by Nigel J. Clarke
John Fowles by Peter Conradi (a critical study of John Fowles's work). Published by Methuen ('Contemporary Writers' series), 1982

On the Track of the Rabbits of Watership Down

Watership Down by Richard Adams
First published by Rex Collings 1972
Penguin paperback, 1973

(White Hill car park — Watership Down — Caesar's Belt and the Portway — Court Drove — the Harroway — Efrafa — Lynch. A high-level walk by tracks, lanes and a short stretch of road which can be done in two short sections of two and a half and two miles [a car is needed to bridge the gap]; as a walk of about seven miles, in one direction only so return transport is needed; or as a round walk of about fifteen miles. Younger walkers might appreciate either of the first two alternatives.)

O.S.– 1:50,000 Sheets No. 174 'Newbury & Wantage' and 185 'Winchester and Basingstoke'
1:25,000 First Series Sheets No. SU 45 'Lichfield' and SU 55 'Kingsclere'

When Richard Adams retired from the Civil Service in 1974, fame had already claimed him as a rather unlikely victim. Several years before, he had put down on paper a story which he had made up to distract his two daughters from the boredom of a long car journey. He had set the tale in a part of the country that he and his wife knew well and loved — the long line of chalk downs on the Berkshire–Hampshire border which rise in a great curving rampart from the valley of the River Kennet and face north towards the Vale of the White Horse.

The simple tale that Richard Adams wove for his daughters around the lives and adventures of the rabbits of Watership Down grew into a full-length 'grown-up novel for children'. When it eventually found a publisher and saw the light of day in 1972, the 52-year-old civil servant found he had hit the jackpot.

Opposite: *Richard Adams*

The Carnegie Medal and the *Guardian* Award for children's fiction were only the start of an avalanche of world-wide acclaim for *Watership Down* that left Richard Adams bemused and rather amused. It also enabled him to retire from his job and give himself up to writing. More books followed, including *Shardik, The Plague Dogs* and *The Girl in a Swing*, each one drawing on Adams's creative flair and powers of description, capturing the thoughts, motives and instincts of both humans and animals. The enormously successful cartoon film of *Watership Down* confirmed the popularity of his first story with people of all ages.

Richard Adams weathered the whirlwind experience of sudden fame and the attention of the world's news media. He lectured at American universities, and took on the presidency of the RSPCA for two rather stormy years — the animal rights movement found it had a champion of independent spirit who was apt to speak his mind without fear or favour.

Richard Adams still best enjoys the gentle country pursuits — folk-song, fly-fishing, walking, bird-watching, beer and shove-ha'penny — of a man who loves to be immersed in rural England. From the first page of *Watership Down*, the minute details of the countryside surround the reader: plants, insects, smells, weather effects, textures of grass and earth. It is a rabbit's-eye view of the world, sustained faultlessly through the long and exciting tale of flight, danger by flood and field, heroism, tyranny, death and re-birth. As well as bringing the natural world alive in all its fine detail, Richard Adams is also a masterful story-teller. The reader is gripped and rushed along by the narrative, which breaks into two main parts. The first deals with the flight of the rabbits from their doomed warren at Sandleford and their perilous journey across several miles of country to the 'high, lonely hills' foreseen by Fiver, the mystic rabbit whose brother, Hazel, is the leader of the band. Here, on Watership Down, they excavate a new warren and try to steal some tame does from the nearby Nuthanger Farm. The failure of this plan leads to the second part of the story, in which the rabbits make another journey to entice does away from the lapine dictatorship of Efrafa, run by the fearsome giant rabbit General Woundwort and his Gestapo-like subordinates. Some of the scenes in this second half of the book — in particular the pursuit of the Efrafan escapers by General Woundwort in a thunderstorm, and the reprisal raid on the warren at Watership Down — must rank among the most exciting sequences in all children's literature.

One of Adams's greatest achievements is to maintain the reader's belief in the rabbits — who can speak, reason and plan, and who possess active imaginations, a strong religious heritage and a full range of emotions — as ordinary, everyday rabbits. He presents them realistically, not sentimentally, influenced by weather, mating urges, their own physical strengths and weaknesses and the ever-present danger from 'elil' — their thousand enemies who are always one pounce away.

*   *   *

Although the route of the rabbits can be followed from Sandleford Warren through Watership Down as far as Efrafa and beyond, it makes for a walk of at least twelve miles, more than some junior walkers can manage — and this is an ideal outing for young *Watership Down* enthusiasts.

Our walk begins at Watership Down itself, from where there is a grand view over the country towards Sandleford. The route from Watership Down to Efrafa is about six miles long — if return transport from Overton is not available, then another eight or nine miles should be allowed for the journey back. Alternatively there is a fine walk of about two and a half miles from the White Hill car park up to the beech hanger on Watership Down and back; after which one could drive via the B3051 to Overton, turn right onto the B3400 and take the second turning on the right to the hamlet of Lynch. Turn left at the T-junction immediately after the bridge over the river Test to reach Northington Farm and the track to Efrafa, one mile to the north. This lets younger walkers have a double bite at the cherry!

One and a half miles south of Kingsclere, the B3051 swings right to climb up the face of the escarpment. Half-way up on the left is White Hill car park, near a tall communications mast (517565). Directly opposite on the right of the road a chalk-white path mounts over the shoulder of the hill. You pass through a white-painted metal gate to join the track at a green wooden fingerpost marked *'Inkpen Beacon 12'*. The track forms part of the long-distance Wayfarers' Walk which follows old rights of way from Emsworth, north of Portsmouth, to the neolithic long barrow on Inkpen Beacon. Remains of ancient man, his burial grounds and high-level paths are all around you on this walk, which follows the course of green roads that have been trodden across the tops of the downs for two thousand years at least.

Nowadays race-horses are exercised on the cinder-surfaced gallops up here, while the long straight chalk tracks that cross the plain below release spiralling clouds of chalk dust behind the speeding farmers' vehicles. Sheep graze the short downland turf, and larks sing. The breeze is fresh and invigorating, and can be very cold, even on a sunny day. The view is stupendous — fifteen or twenty miles at least, across Newbury towards the Thames and the North Berkshire Downs. There is one jarring note in the peaceful rural scene — the squarish blocks of the Greenham Common air-base, clearly visible to the east of Newbury, where cruise missiles lie in their heavily guarded silos.

Opposite: *The beech wood, Watership Down*
Below: *Bigwig's tree, Watership Down*

The path heads straight for the long, thin beech wood at the crest of Watership Down that comes up the slope of the south-facing land and stops a few yards short of the path and the edge of the escarpment (499569). Two big beeches stand sentinel at the north-east corner of the wood, one with a semi-circle of horse-shoes nailed round a hole in its hollow trunk and the name ·BIGWIG· carved by some admirer into the bark. Bigwig was the dashing, strong and impulsive rabbit who joined the fugitives from the Sandleford Warren at the start of the story, and who learned to accept the leadership of the quieter and gentler but more perceptive Hazel. Somewhere close by is the spot where the rabbits dug the 'Honeycomb', a great central chamber with the roots of the trees for a support, surrounded by a system of burrows and runs.

Beyond the edge of the wood is a hedge of stunted thorns, and then the smooth shoulder of grass that rolls to the sudden drop of the escarpment. Here is a perfect place to sit and admire the marvellous view. Directly below is the straight track that runs between fields over a low ridge to Nuthanger Farm (499585), whose roofs are just visible. Nuthanger Farm features in two thrilling episodes in the book. It is the scene of the abortive raid when Hazel led five of the rabbits in an attempt to get four tame does out of a hutch in the farmer's shed. The expedition ended with only two of the does reaching the Honeycomb on Watership Down, and with Hazel shot and almost killed by the farmer's men. The second incident is at the climax of the book, when Hazel returns to the farm to lure a dog up the hill in the nick of time to fall on the Efrafans in their moment of victory. In the cartoon film this is a splendidly bloody and shocking piece of action.

The line of 'iron trees' or pylons marches away across the foreground into the distance beyond Kingsclere, while over to the left lie the copses and fields between Watership Down and the little river Enborne. Here the rabbits encountered a dog on their first night out from the Sandleford Warren, and crossed the river (472639) using a piece of wood which Blackberry's intelligence transformed into a raft.

From this superb viewpoint the walk continues as a grassy path over the down towards Ladle Hill, the next promontory on the escarpment, which is crowned by an Iron Age fort

(479568), only half completed by its builders, one of a string of such forts which utilized the natural advantage provided by the escarpment. However, our route does not follow the more obvious of the paths that heads for Ladle Hill, but curves south-west and then south round the top of the rabbits' wood. It keeps close to the hedge on the left, passing between two tumuli (one well defined on the open grassland, the other masked by trees beyond the hedge) well to the left of the triangulation pillar in the field ahead. You go over a gate between two stiles (496567) and keep to the edge of the next field, with a fence on your left. The views are far and wide, of rolling, pylon-dotted countryside that undulates away in waves of grassy ridges clothed with hedges and trees. Chalk and flints show through the soil, which supports tattered hedges of old thorn bushes.

Cannon Heath Farm, in the valley below on your left, sends horses up to stretch their legs and lungs on the gallops of Watership Down. You cross the track to the farm and continue along the rutted path between thick thorn hedges, under crackling electricity wires towards the long line of Caesar's Belt, a three-mile strip of larch, beech and hazel that marks the line of a Roman road, the Portway. It ran from Silchester to Old Sarum, two miles north of present-day Salisbury, and was an important link in the system of communications that those ingenious road-builders established in south England. It may well have been a Roman road-improvement scheme rather than something they actually planned themselves: some experts believe that the Portway was laid down along the route of a Bronze Age road, and that the Romans simply adapted what was already there.

Nowadays the Portway wears many disguises — everything from a first-class road to a hedgerow track — but its arrow-straight course is plain to see crossing the Ordnance Survey maps. You cross it where it leaves the road and runs through Caesar's Belt as a raised causeway about one foot high and twelve to fifteen feet wide (501544). A few yards further south is the straight road where you turn right for five hundred yards and then go left where the road bends right, onto the tarmac side-road marked *Willesley Warren Farm* (500537).

Opposite the entrance to the side-road is a gate from which

you can look back at Caesar's Belt and the spinney which clings
to its southern side. A party of rabbits from Watership Down,
led as usual by Hazel, rested in the spinney on their way to
Efrafa and the second doe-stealing adventure. One of the
treats of *Watership Down* is the selection of stories from the
rabbits' folklore that breaks up the narrative from time to time.
Most concern El-Ahrairah, the impudent Prince of Rabbits,
and his resourceful lieutenant Rabscuttle — two very English
Brer Rabbits, always in trouble and invariably getting out of it
with a piece of daring or downright cheek. That evening in the
spinney, Dandelion told the story of El-Ahrairah and the
Black Rabbit of Inlé, a grim figure of doom before whom all
rabbits must bow — even El-Ahrairah. The story was
interrupted by a fox, whom Bigwig, in a moment of typical
impulsiveness, went out to meet and draw off in the combe
below the spinney. Bigwig, fortunately for himself, led the fox
on to a patrol of rabbits from Efrafa, and one of their number
paid the price of Bigwig's foolhardy piece of daring.

The Watership Down rabbits made their way to Efrafa by
fields and woods to the right of our route — rabbits observe no

Looking north towards Efrafa

rights of way, unlike human walkers! However, the road that you tread is an ancient drove road, Court Drove, that leads past Willesley Warren Farm and on for another mile, utterly peaceful, remote and secluded. The high land stretches away in all directions, and the path becomes more grassy and softer underfoot with every step. In a 360° skyscape every kind of weather can be present at one time — bright sunlight on the path, clouds shadowing the next field and shafts of rain falling on the field beyond that. This is ancient country where tumuli abound and where neolithic axes and Roman pottery are unearthed by the plough.

About a mile beyond Willesley Warren Farm the path is crossed by a winding lane in a tunnel of trees (505515), down which you turn to the right. Old-man's-beard smothers the ivy-covered trees each side of the lane. Some of these trees look as if they have been standing there for many centuries — but the lane itself is many times older than the oldest tree. This is the Harroway, known to the Saxons as the Hoare or Ancient Way, a neolithic route which is probably the oldest road in Britain. It is a continuation of the Pilgrim's Way, which starts at Canterbury, from west of Guildford to Salisbury Plain — and may well have pursued its winding course through Devon and Cornwall to the tin mines at Marazion, a few miles from the westernmost tip of Britain. Tin, a vital component in the manufacture of bronze, would have been distributed to consumers all along the south coast by means of this trade route, now shrunk to a meandering and neglected lane.

After three-quarters of a mile the Harroway is crossed by a lane from New Barn (498508). Richard Adams names this spot the Crixa, and in the woods on each side he sited Efrafa, the dictatorship ruled by General Woundwort. The reader is forced to admire this swaggering bully, who has organized his warren so efficiently that no rabbit dare raise a murmur of dissent and each shift or 'mark' lives its daily life to a strict timetable. Obedience, punishment and oppression are the order in Efrafa, until Bigwig joins up and starts to spread subversion among the young does. Helped by the Watership Down rabbits' good friend Kehaar, a seagull with a fine line in bad language, Bigwig at last breaks cover and in a fearful thunderstorm leads a party of dissenters from Efrafa down the field to the south of the trees towards the 'iron road' or railway line on its embankment at the bottom of the slope.

From the Crixa, turn left down the lane from New Barn. The gate on the right leads into the field, where many rabbit burrows are to be seen along the edge of the wood on the site of Efrafa — though the rabbits that scurry for cover with a white flash of scut at the sight of a walker look independent enough!

Follow the lane down to the bridge over the railway (500501). In the centre of the embankment a couple of hundred yards to your right is the 'roadless railway arch' (497500) where Hazel and the other Watership Down rabbits waited in the storm for Bigwig and the escaping Efrafan does. Chalk drawings of Kehaar, Bigwig and the 'crack-brained slave-driver' Woundwort adorn the inner walls of the arch, as do signatures of all the rabbits, and messages scrawled there by *Watership Down* devotees. Some have obviously followed the trail of the rabbits all the way from Sandleford. All the graffiti are mercifully innocent — none of the *Efrafa United Are Hraka* variety.

In the field beyond the arch, Kehaar attacked the General and gained enough time for the rabbits to get down to the bank of the river Test, which flows through the woods at the bottom of the field. Unfortunately this is all private property, so walkers are not able to reach the scene of Woundwort's defeat by the bridge (498494), where the Watership Down rabbits floated away with his does on a punt in front of his flabbergasted face. General Woundwort, however, could not stomach the insult or the injury, and mounted the final raid on Watership Down in which he disappeared — perhaps to meet the Black Rabbit of Inlé, perhaps to fresh fields and pastures new.

To gain the B3400 road, continue down the track from the railway bridge to Northington Farm (501497), turn left and walk by the many-channelled Test to the hamlet of Lynch. Turn right to cross the river and reach the road (507495).

If you have not arranged transport back to White Hill car park, an eight-mile return walk can be made by turning right along the B3400 through Laverstoke, turning right again into the lane just past the church (486488). Cross the railway line and bear right into the long lane to Twinley (484500). Turn left at the T-junction (480519), and then, after about half a mile, right into the lane that winds up through Caesar's Belt and passes Hare Warren Farm and Ashley Warren Farm. Half a mile further on, turn right up a short track (492562) which meets the path back to the rabbits' wood on Watership Down.

Information on Local History and Walking
Basingstoke Archaeological and Historical Society, 31, Winchester Street, Overton, Basingstoke, Hants RG25 3HT
Basingstoke Ramblers' Club, 67, Cumberland Avenue, Basingstoke, Hants

Local Library
19–20, Westminster House, Potters Walk, Basingstoke, Hants RG21 1LS

A Gallop with the Scarecrow on Romney Marsh

The Further Adventures of Doctor Syn
by Russell Thorndike
First published by Rich and Cowan, 1936

(The Ship Inn, Dymchurch — New Hall — Orgarswick Farm — Burmarsh — Abbott's Court Farm — The Royal Military Canal — Lympne Castle — West Hythe — Botolph's Bridge — New Beach Holiday Centre — Dymchurch. About ten miles, by field paths and lanes. A walk best done in dry weather. Careful navigation is needed in places; some footbridges across dykes are hidden in reeds, and some are very narrow.)

O.S.– 1:50,000 Sheet No. 189 'Ashford and Romney Marsh'
1:25,000 Sheets No. TR 01/02 'New Romney and Dungeness,
TR 03 'Aldington (Kent)' and TR 13/23 'Folkestone and Hythe'

Outside the Ship Inn at Dymchurch, two men are fighting desperately with duelling rapiers. One, a swaggering, black-bearded bully in an eighteenth-century naval officer's uniform, is cheered on by a villainous crew of sailors; his opponent, in a dragoon officer's red coat of the same period, is backed by fellow dragoons, tankards in hand. Round the characters a semi-circular crowd of five hundred onlookers encourages the handsome young dragoon. At last the bully goes down, the dragoon's rapier embedded in his chest. The old white-bearded village doctor appears, administers a pill, and the bully springs up, bows to the audience, and goes off into the public bar of the Ship, arm in arm with his antagonist. Meanwhile, a bent-backed and gap-toothed sexton is leering at his master, the saintly-looking vicar of Dymchurch, while more onlookers jockey for good camera shots of the pair outside Mr Mipps' Coffin Shop. Later in the day the dragoons will be down on Dymchurch Beach, being hurled into puddles

Opposite: *Russell Thorndike in his study at Mortlake*

The Dymchurch 'Day of Syn' — Smugglers with contraband

of sea-water by a gang of cut-throat smugglers from a fleet of fishing boats landing tubs of contraband brandy.

It is the 'Day of Syn' — a biennial day of fun and profit for local charities, when Dymchurch residents take on the outward forms of the main characters from a series of books now largely forgotten by the outside world, but still read avidly here on Romney Marsh at the outermost corner of Kent — the Doctor Syn saga. Every other August Bank Holiday Monday there rides again the blandly smiling Doctor Christopher Syn, conscientious parson by day and notorious smuggler — 'The Scarecrow' — by night, accompanied by the other characters from the seven Doctor Syn books. Local interest has grown so rapidly in the twenty years since the first 'Day of Syn' that the little village under the sea wall is crammed with many thousands of visitors. Television and local radio have featured the event: afterwards the local papers are full of it. Yet the books are now out of print, only obtainable in second-hand shops around the towns of Romney Marsh or in the nearby public libraries.

They were the creations of Russell Thorndike, brother of the celebrated actress Dame Sybil Thorndike and himself a noted actor in his day. He was born on 6th February 1885, the son of a canon of Rochester Cathedral, and spent much of his childhood making up and performing plays with Sybil. They were devotedly attached to each other all through their long lives. Russell went to St George's School in Windsor, where for a period he was Queen Victoria's boy soloist. In 1903 he and Sybil were both at Ben Greet's famous acting academy, and by the time the First World War broke out they had both established themselves on the stage, in spite of a remark made about Russell by Greet's colleague, Frederick Topham: ' . . . odd and unexpected; I think he should be a clown.'

Russell and Sybil had toured the world by 1914, and Russell had written the first book in the Doctor Syn saga, in a coastguard's cottage at Dymchurch. From childhood the Thorndikes had holidayed on Romney Marsh, and Russell in particular had fallen in love with its wildness, remoteness, and character completely unlike any other part of England. Marshmen were — and still are — proud of their independence, their special local laws and dialect, and their ruler-flat landscape scored and criss-crossed by drainage ditches. Russell took the fiercely independent local character and the isolated, cut-off surroundings of 'Dymchurch-under-the-Wall', mixed them with a strong dash of more or less accurate smuggling history, and created the devil-may-care smuggler, the Scarecrow, who rode his fierce black stallion, Gehenna, across the marshes at night, with his lieutenants, Hellspite (Mipps the Sexton by day) and Beelzebub (Jimmie Bone the highwayman — an actual figure from local history who terrorized coaches on the Dover Road), directing his Night Riders with their tubs of brandy, and defying dragoons, local magistrates, traitors, rivals, Bow Street Runners and bounty hunters with panache and daring. By day, of course, the Scarecrow became the gentle and respectable Doctor Syn, vicar of Dymchurch-under-the-Wall, Dean of the Peculiars of Romney Marsh and sworn enemy to the Scarecrow.

The seven books in the series are certainly not great literature, but they are all rattling good yarns, swashbuckling tales written with dash and inventiveness by someone obviously relishing his subject. Russell had killed off Doctor Syn in the first book, *Doctor Syn — a tale of the Romney Marsh*, which came out in 1915; and the rest of the saga had to predate the original book. The story unfolds from the stealing of Syn's beautiful young wife by a dastardly villain, which forces the parson to turn pirate in order to find her again. From the moment of his return in the wreck of a gale-tossed brig, the marsh rings by night to demon yells, shots, the clash of swords and the thunder of spectral hooves, and by day to the equally thunderous curses of General Troubridge, the commander of dragoons at Dover Castle, and splenetic Sir Henry Pembury, Lord of Lympne Castle and Scarecrowphobe. This heady brew of out-and-out adventure proved ideal for the stage — Russell himself played the title part — and the cinema; three versions have been made to date. However, Russell hardly made a penny out of the success of his creation, and continued to tread the boards for the rest of his active life.

He had been badly wounded in 1915 at Gallipoli, coming back to England with a dislocated spine, depressed and bent nearly double. This injury resulted in his being invalided out of the army, and he joined Sybil at the Old Vic in 1916, playing many leading Shakespeare roles, such as Hamlet, King Lear and Richard II. After the war, he helped to start up a Grand Guignol theatre of horror in London, getting involved in grisly scenes where he was frightened to death in a waxworks exhibition, eaten by wolfhounds and, in one play, put out the eyes of the character played by Sybil. Audiences stormed out in disgust, one man was sick all over the mat in the theatre foyer, and the reviewers were aghast. After this experiment, which perfectly suited Russell's taste for the shocking and macabre, he went on to play Peer Gynt and Hamlet, and subsequently take roles that brought him less and less satisfaction.

Russell's name became a by-word for eccentricity. He was supposed to have queued up 'to see this fellow Thorndike who they all say is so good'. Ordinary events became romantic adventures in the telling, and he especially delighted in holding children spellbound with his fantastic stories. John Casson said of him: 'He lives and breathes in a world not of make-believe but of reality wildly and often madly intensified by his own bouncing imagination. I defy anyone ever to be bored in Russell's company.'

He continued to enjoy hamming it up in improvised charades with Sybil and other friends, but once he had ceased to be a pioneer the stage held fewer attractions for him. The Doctor Syn saga really took off in 1935, when the second title appeared, *Doctor Syn Returns*. This was followed by *Doctor Syn on the High Seas* and *The Further Adventures of Doctor Syn* (both 1936), *The Amazing Quest of Doctor Syn* (1938), *The Courageous Exploits of Doctor Syn* (1939), and finally, *The Shadow of Doctor Syn* (1944). Some written for enjoyment, some — with Sybil's help — to raise money when funds were low, the books kept Russell's name before the public. Modern tough novels of sex and violence had not yet put their swashbuckling style out of court.

Russell Thorndike died at the great age of eighty-seven, on 7th November 1972.

The Further Adventures of Doctor Syn takes place wholly on Romney Marsh, and can claim to be the best of the Doctor Syn books. The common theme that links his various adventures is the parson's black-list of enemies, who are cut down to size one by one. The Scarecrow allows himself to be captured by General Troubridge's faithful side-kick, Major Faunce, only to escape from the tower cell at Dover Castle in apparently supernatural circumstances. Again, he gives himself up to Cornet Brackenbury in order to help the young dragoon win the hand of Kate Pembury, the daughter of the cantankerous Lord of Lympne Castle; this time Sir Henry Pembury ends up lashed to the Dymchurch gibbet post with the inscription: *A laughing stock, by order of the Scarecrow*.

Mr Fragg, a government agent sent from London to break up the smuggling gang, is discovered dead one morning in the mud banks of a sluice, while Farmer Brazlett, the informer who had provided a list of gang members, is hanged at his own farewell party in the Dymchurch tithe barn. The rival Bonnington Gang, delivered up to justice by the Scarecrow, are reprieved by him as a salutary lesson to them. A French privateer is captured by the Scarecrow, who then steals it under the noses of the Navy; the unpleasant duellist Captain

Raikes gets a taste of his own medicine; a murderer is cleverly murdered in his turn; a Bow Street Runner is run to earth; a press-gang is pressed and returned to duty packed in barrels; a gang of horse-thieves is punished by transportation to France in the Scarecrow's own vessel. Our Romney Marsh ramble starts, however, at the Ship Inn, Sexton Mipps' favourite watering-hole.

* * *

In Doctor Syn's day the main A259 Rye to Hythe road ran round the back of the Ship Inn (104298) — hence the back-to-front appearance of the building, whose main entrance faces away from the road. Sexton Mipps' Coffin Shop stands beside the Inn, now advertising its trade in lunches and teas in deliberately mis-spelt capitals. From his work knocking up coffins for the parish, the little sexton was only a few strides away from his noggin of rum in the bar presided over by Mrs Waggetts, who would ask him to step over and cast his eye on suspicious strangers, such as Mr Fragg, the government agent. To the Ship Inn came Stubbard the pressgang leader with his group of thugs, searching for the young men of Dymchurch; but Mrs Waggetts and Mipps between them managed to foil him. Nowadays the Ship Inn is the centre of the Day of Syn activities, and the most popular pub of the three in Dymchurch. The other two, the City of London and the Ocean, feature in the saga; the Ocean overlooks the dismal, mud-choked sluice of scummy green water where Fragg met his untimely end.

From the main road entrance to the Ship, you cross over the road and walk down the lane between the church and New Hall. New Hall, on your left, dates from 1574, and is a large, square, red-brick building with tiled roofs. Today it is the Romney Marsh Local Government Administration Centre, as it was in Doctor Syn's day. Here Sir Antony Cobtree, the Squire of Dymchurch, dispensed summary justice to local smugglers. In front of it, where the War Memorial stands, was the village gibbet where many of those malefactors ended their lives—unpleasantly near the Vicarage, as Dr Syn remarked to Sir Henry Pembury. The old prison cell with its solid, narrow wooden door, can still be seen built into the north-western wall of the court-house.

Sir Antony himself probably lived just down the main road at the Old Manor House next door to the present Vicarage. No trace remains of Doctor Syn's Vicarage, though it probably stood on the same site as the large Victorian one just beyond the court-house. Opposite these two handsome buildings is the Church of St Peter and St Paul, built of rough stone blocks, roughly clad with weather-proof mortar, with a small square tower and a weather vane whose design of sword and cross-keys looks just like a Jolly Roger. A Norman arch leads into an interior altered and extended sideways in late Georgian times, but with its gallery still in existence. In front of the altar, hidden under a carpet, is a memorial slab to a Riding Officer contemporary with those who persecuted the Scarecrow's Night Riders.

Continue past the Vicarage and the Church Hall, and cross an ancient little red-brick bridge over a dyke (102297) where a green signpost points you onwards to Orgarswick. Ahead are fields completely flat, studded with wind-blown trees and bushes, and separated by drainage dykes. The whole of the marsh was under water when the Romans came to this part of the world, a great bay dotted with muddy islands. The line of hills ahead, which marks the extremity of the North Downs, was at that time a line of cliffs with the sea lapping their feet. The Romans built a fortified wall at Dymchurch to keep the ocean at bay, but it was the monks that followed them who began to reclaim the land from the sea, making walls and drainage ditches which gradually won back the silt-enriched ground for farming. Drainage has been constantly improved over the centuries, the royal will being brought to bear around the time of the Crusades in creating elected 'Jurats' to see that the sea was properly kept at bay and the land drained and exploited more efficiently. Nowadays the Romney Marsh soil grows almost anything that is planted there, and the farmers are the envy of Kent. Fat Romney Marsh sheep graze, heads down, on the salty grass.

You cross the diminutive 15-inch gauge rails of the Romney, Hythe and Dymchurch Railway. The hoarse whistling of its scaled-down engines can be heard all over the marsh, and the course of the railway followed by the plumes of smoke from their funnels. One of them is appropriately named *Dr Syn*. Carry on in a straight line through field gates with a reed-choked dyke on your left, the outbuildings of Orgarswick Farm dead ahead, and the low outline of the village of Burmarsh with its church tower away to the right. At the end of the first field beyond the railway, go over the stile in front of you (not the gate to the left) and cross the dyke by a plank bridge. Bear left round the edge of the next field, and cross the dyke on your left by a single-plank bridge with a hand rail half-hidden in the reeds (098302). Turn right with the dyke now on your right, and follow the edge of the field to a T-junction of dykes. Turn left here, and continue to follow the field edge along until you cross the dyke by a solid causeway. Now keep straight ahead to join a farm road which runs up to Orgarswick Farm (090309).

Here came Mr Fragg, piloted by Sexton Mipps, to see Hugh Brazlett, the 'pattern parishioner' with the list of 57 smugglers' names. Russell Thorndike did not positively place Brazlett's farm, but it was 'Burmarsh way' and 'a tricky farm to find' — both of these descriptions fit Orgarswick. The house now stands at the edge of a large complex of corrugated-iron outbuildings, but beside it is a small red-brick outhouse which corresponds to the disused wash-house which Brazlett used as an office and at whose drain-hole the intrepid Mipps eavesdropped, full-length in the snow outside, as the farmer made his fatal deal with the 'foreigner'.

From Orgarswick Farm continue along the tarmac road for fifty yards, then turn right down a well-marked track. There is a pretty view ahead of the white and red houses of Burmarsh with the church tower peeping from a clump of trees in the middle. The track brings you across the fields to the Burmarsh road just below Forty Acre Cottage (093319). Turn right here to reach Burmarsh.

All Saints Church, a small, grey stone battlemented building, is reached by a little bridge over a drainage ditch. The Norman door has a fine gargoyle leering down in a gap-toothed grin from the top of the arch.

Turn left by the Shepherd and Crook pub and follow the road up to Abbott's Court Farm (102328). Now the line of the inland cliffs is much nearer, and Lympne Castle can be seen clearly amongst its trees high up to the right. Go straight through the farmyard to the gate into the field beyond. Bear left around the edge of this field to a gate and stile, and steer straight ahead towards the red roofs of Port Lympne, a very successful wildlife park run by John Aspinall, set in the woods that face the flat lands below. On reaching the road, turn left, and immediately right again down Aldergate Lane to the line of trees that marks the Royal Military Canal.

This is the most notable remnant of the many anti-invasion devices that litter Romney Marsh, always a prime target for a cross-Channel invader by virtue of its proximity to the Continent and its flat, easily negotiated terrain. In the vicinity of Dymchurch are several Martello towers, sturdy strongholds built against Napoleon; and the Royal Military Canal is also an anti-Boney measure. It was begun in 1804 in response to the massing of invasion barges in the channel ports across the water. The original design was a dry ditch, built in horizontal steps so that cannon sited at the bottom of each section would have a clear field of fire along the next section of ditch. It runs

The Royal Military Canal

from Pett Level below Rye right around the top of the marsh to Hythe, separating the whole area from the inland cliffs behind it. By 1805, when Napoleon had abandoned his plans to invade England, the digging of the canal was well under way. Once having gained momentum, the construction work simply carried on, though now totally without purpose. Four years and nearly a quarter of a million pounds later it was finished — a splendid and lovely but militarily useless water-course, nowadays dappled with kingcups and fringed with fishermen.

Cross the canal by the bridge (101343) and turn right onto the narrow bridle path (signposted) that runs among the trees on the north bank. For more than a mile you walk along in a tunnel of green foliage — willows and elm suckers beginning to regenerate after the ravages of Dutch elm disease — with glimpses of the hillside on your left between the trees. Suddenly there is a gap in the trees, and you look up at the ruins of Stutfall Castle, built by the Romans to guard their harbour of Portus Lemanis. All that remains of the twenty-foot high walls of the castle are great lumps of masonry in a tussocky field, below the towers, roofs and chimneys of Lympne Castle on the heights above and behind. A Roman soldier from Stutfall is said to haunt Lympne Castle.

Here at a public-footpath stone you leave the trees, cross the dyke by a footbridge (116341) and zig-zag up the hill on a well-trodden footpath. You are rewarded at the top with a superb view over the whole of Romney Marsh spread out below you, rectangular fields, winding roads, gleaming dykes, isolated houses and small villages, and the wide ribbon of the Royal Military Canal making its way to Hythe and the sea. Hythe was one of the Cinque Ports established by Edward the Confessor — the others were Hastings, Romney, Dover and Sandwich — to which five Rye and Winchelsea were later added — which, in return for various legal and financial favours, were expected to furnish and maintain between them a navy capable of beating off any attacks on the vulnerable marshland. They fattened on the privileges, and by the thirteenth century had become the centre of a mighty trading and defence confederacy all along this coast, which fought many bloody sea-battles with the French. The Cinque Ports were attacked, burned and swept by plagues at various times, but it was the gentle, inexorable silting up and shifting of sea and land watercourses that finally broke their power. Romney, Winchelsea and Rye are all now landlocked and their prosperity comes from tourism; the other four thrive on the holiday trade or cross-Channel transport.

After admiring the panorama, turn right and make for Lympne Castle (119347) — open to the public in the summer months — which was built in about 1360 as a further safeguard and stronghold. The path passes the massive gateway of the Castle, which is really a complex of fortifications and houses built up into a homogeneous unit. Here we pick up the Dr Syn connection again, for Lympne Castle was the home of Sir Henry Pembury, the gout-ridden old dandy who challenged the Squire of Dymchurch, Sir Antony Cobtree, to a duel in the great dining-hall of the Castle. Sir Antony laughed off the challenge, upon which Sir Henry, after venting some of his spleen with his riding crop on his stable-hands, was goaded into vowing to young Cornet Brackenbury: 'the day you bring this infamous Scarecrow into this room, bound, and hand him over to me as my prisoner you shall marry my daughter out of hand if she is free.' Unfortunately the saintly Vicar of Dymchurch was a witness to this promise; and, as the Scarecrow, forced Sir Henry to keep his vow while making a laughing-stock of him at Dymchurch gibbet post.

The path passes the churchyard of Lympne Church, part of the Castle complex, between tall beech trees, goes through a gate, and in fifty yards leaves the road to the right by old stone steps (122347) that take you down across a field to the edge of a wood. Follow this down to the road, turning right there to descend the hill to West Hythe, a straggling village from which the road enters the familiar flat marshland around Botolph's Bridge (121335). The inn by the bridge was a famous smugglers' haunt in the time of King George III, and many a run was planned in its back kitchens. Smuggling was a major activity on the Marsh, gangs of several hundred men often being necessary for purchase of the tubs of brandy or other contraband on the Continent, loading and transportation to England, landing the cargo on the marsh beaches and carrying it from there to specially prepared hides in farmyards, cellars or attics. Wool, a valuable and highly taxable commodity, often made its way in the opposite direction. Although Russell Thorndike romanticized the smuggling gangs, they were in fact by the late eighteenth century the terror of the neighbourhood, run by bloodthirsty and utterly ruthless men, and often only immune from prosecution through fear of Mafia-style reprisals on informers — such as Doctor Syn's treatment of Mr Fragg. The Riding Officers did their best to combat the smuggling menace and to win the proper dues for the Government, but there were far too few of them, and the law breakers carried on until the smuggling died out in the nineteenth century — at least on such a scale!

The present-day inn sign at Botolph's Bridge shows a rather ambiguous scene in bas-relief. Four monks are carrying the body of St Botolph across the Marsh on its final journey from Winchester to Canterbury Cathedral, guided by a heavenly light — but they look suspiciously like four smugglers carrying a tub of brandy over the bridge by the light of a signal beacon!

Two scenes in *The Further Adventures of Doctor Syn* are set at Botolph's Bridge. One is an attack by the Tankerton horse-thieving gang on two Night Riders. The other is one of the best scenes in the book, in which the arrogant duellist Captain Raikes goes to Botolph's Bridge at dead of night to fight Kate Pembury's new husband, Cornet Brackenbury, with whom he has deliberately picked a quarrel in order to get his hands on the young bride over her husband's dead body. Before the duel, Brackenbury says 'a prayer towards the distant heights of Lympne, where in the Castle slept his young adorable wife, little realizing that her husband was about to go to death, unless the Scarecrow could perform a miracle'.

Needless to say, the miracle occurs, and the unconscious body of the bully is delivered to Dover Castle next day, buried in a cart-load of vegetables, with his broken sword beside him.

Somewhere in the neighbourhood of Botolph's Bridge was the isolated cottage of Mother Handaway, the old witch who stabled Gehenna for the Scarecrow and Jimmy Bone's horse for that suave gentleman of the road.

Turn down the Dymchurch road from the bridge, and in fifty yards cross a stile on the left at a public footpath sign. Go diagonally over the field to a plank footbridge with a tubular guard-rail over a dyke (120332), and continue across the fields, keeping about twenty yards between you and the dyke on your left. You cross another dyke, and with a fence on your right walk towards the Romney, Hythe and Dymchurch railway line, which you cross where it runs over the dyke (116319). The flat fields around you are several feet below sea-level, only saved from inundation by the great sea wall at Dymchurch.

Walk on along the right-hand bank of the dyke to the next bridge, where the footpath to Dymchurch has been obliterated by the farmer. Turn left here down a track which ends at the sprawling complex of the New Beach Holiday Centre.

At the main road turn right for a hundred yards, and climb the steps to the top of the sea wall for a two-mile walk above the beach back to the Ship Hotel and Sexton Mipps' Coffin Shop.

The Dymchurch Day of Syn
c/o Mrs Coral Fowler (Hon. Secretary), 19 Kingsway, Dymchurch, Kent.
The Day of Syn takes place in alternate years (*odd* numbers e.g. 1985, 1987).

Local Library
Central Library, Grace Hill, Folkestone, Kent

Useful books
Romney Marsh by Richard Ingrams and Fay Godwin. Published by Wildwood House, 1980
The Cinque Ports and Romney Marsh by Margaret Brentnall. Published by John Gifford Ltd, 1980
Romney Marsh by Walter Murray. Published by Robert Hale, 3rd edition 1982
Honest Thieves by F.E. Nicholls (a good general book on smuggling). Published by Heinemann, 1973

A Prodigious Fine Walk
with Parson Woodforde

The Diary of a Country Parson 1758–1802
by James Woodforde, edited by John Beresford
Oxford University Press paperback, 1978

(Weston Longville — Lyng — Lenwade Bridge — Weston Longville. A straightforward walk of about six and a half miles by footpaths and lanes)

O.S.– 1:50,000 Sheet No. 133 'North East Norfolk'
       1:25,000 Sheets No. TG 11 'Attlebridge' and No. TG 01 'Hockering'

'We had for Dinner to day one Fowl boiled and Piggs face, a Couple of Rabbitts smothered with Onions, a Piece of rost Beef and some Grape Tarts. . . I went out with my Man this morning tracing Hares, we found one fine one which the Dogs killed. At Cribbage this Evening with Nancy won 0.2.0. She was very sulky and sullen on loosing it, tho' not paid. She did not scarce open her Mouth all the Even' after . . . Miss Mary Donne is a very genteel, pretty young Lady and very agreeable with a most pleasing Voice abt. 21 Yrs. very tasty and very fashionable in dress. . . the Frost severer than ever in the night as it even froze the Chamber Pots under the Beds.'

To any admirer these diary extracts will immediately bring one name to mind — that of Parson James Woodforde, who held the living of Weston Longville, near Norwich in Norfolk, from 1776 until his death at the age of sixty-two on New Year's Day, 1803. The day-to-day observations of this obscure country parson are famous the world over, not for their commentary on great affairs — matters such as the French Revolution and the independence of America did not receive the attention a modern diarist would give them — but for the personal and precise picture they give us of that pre-Industrial Revolution

Opposite: *Parson James Woodforde, the post-mortem portrait in Weston Longville Church*

England whose population of about seven million lived almost entirely in small villages and towns, closely linked to agriculture and the natural world.

Life was lived at a slow tempo in a country without railways, reliable roads or any of our modern means of communication. In the villages the squires held sway, some despotically, others benevolently. The doctor and the parson shared their tables and stables, though not their social standing. Gentlemen paid each other visits during which they shot, hunted, fished and ate twenty-dish meals before long card-playing sessions when the smuggled brandy flowed until bewigged heads could take no more. At the bottom of the pile, the great mass of peasantry continued to work on the squire's land in a system little changed from the feudal. Ordinary people's lives were virtually untouched by wars and international upheavals; stability was the keynote. King George III had been on the throne for sixteen years when Parson Woodforde came to Norfolk, and he outlived the parson by seventeen years.

In those tranquil, time-suspended days of the late eighteenth century the Church of England was in a bad way. With large families the rule, and places for the older sons in politics or the army, or at the helm of a country estate, younger sons frequently slipped almost by default into the Church, often with no vocation or aptitude for the job at all. Bishops were mighty men who tended to lead their own lives in palace and cathedral, and left the country clergy to run the parishes much as they liked. Many clergymen spent their time in pleasant social calls, field sports and heavy eating and drinking; others were absentees from their livings for decades at a time, paying young curates to do their work for them. The 1833 Oxford Movement finally revitalized the Church and bred a new kind of country parson — fervent, dedicated and self-consciously ecclesiastical. Their achievements were enormous, especially in the slums of the great new cities and in missionary work overseas; but with all their passion and zeal they lost the simple ties with their neighbours and the land that were natural to the clergymen of Parson Woodforde's day.

James Woodforde was born at Ansford in Somerset on 16th June 1740, the son of the Rector of Ansford and Vicar of Castle Cary. He went to Winchester and New College, Oxford, where he learned to drink and did enough work to get a degree. After he had served in various curacies in Somerset, his uncle bought the Castle Cary living for his own son, Francis, and Woodforde, who had hoped to gain it for himself, went back to New College a sadder and a poorer man. He served there as sub-warden and pro-proctor before being appointed in 1775 to the living of Weston Longville, a place he probably thought of as the outermost back of beyond.

On 24th May 1776 he reached Weston Parsonage with his nephew Bill (a self-centred scapegrace who was always in hot water) and servant Will Coleman (another bad hat, who abused Woodforde when drunk, soon became 'ill in the venereal way', and was finally sacked and reinstated at the lower level of gardener). The parson was a bachelor, having been 'jilted' in 1775 by Miss Betsy White, his 'dear Maid of Shepton', and was joined by his niece, Nancy, who lived with him at the Parsonage until he died. She was the daughter of his reckless brother, Heighes, the father of an illegitimate child as well as several born the right side of the blanket, a drunkard and inveterate borrower of money from the parson. Brother Jack was little better, being inclined to fall off his horse when 'disguised in Beer'.

Parson Woodforde's diary, in plain, exact language, relates all the happenings of each day. Prices are meticulously noted: 'At Mr Bakers for a P^r of large Scissars to trim Horses pd 1.6. At Dittos — for 2 P^d of Pinns for Nancy and Mrs Davy pd 4.8.'

There are cures for the Whirligigousticon or malaria — a Vomit in the Evening, a Rhubarb Draught the following morning, and a decreasing dose of Bark (Quinine) and Laudanum (opium); a superstitious remedy for a stye on the eye-lid — rub it with the tail of a black cat; tasty treatment for Nancy's upset stomach — a half pint of Rum and Water, and a good dose of Rhubarb and Ginger.

There are vivid accounts of festivities: slightly awkward Tithe Audits where the local farmers paid him their dues and filled themselves with his 'rost Beef and Beer'; Bishop Blaize's Grand Procession at Norwich; and New Year's Eve fun and games at the Parsonage. Freaks and oddities, those spicers of dull days, abound — the learned Pigg, a Mongooz from Madagascar, the 'little Woman only 33 Inches high'.

But the diary's greatest treasures are the doings and sayings of Parson Woodforde's people, who come irresistibly to life as you read. Nancy, his niece, so often 'saucy' through the boredom of being a premature old maid; the vulgar, high-spirited widow Mrs Davy, whose garters the diarist captured on the eve of St Valentine's Day, 1781; her naughty daughter, Betsy, who with her hare-brained lover, Mr Walker, led Nancy temporarily astray and made Parson Woodforde's life a misery by uncontrollable giggling; the curates, parsons and squires who exchanged visits with him, chief among them the noble-hearted Squire Custance of Weston House, his wife and their eight children (more died in infancy), who became the parson's generous friends and earned his admiration and affection.

Towards the end of his life Parson Woodforde became ill, depressed and anxious. The Custances left Weston to live at Bath, and Woodforde quarrelled with his neighbours at Witchingham, the odious Mr and Mrs Jeanes. He ceased to go to church, and became more and more obsessed with his ailments — a lonely and crusty old man. When the end came it was a merciful release, both for him and the long-suffering Nancy.

Some aspects of his character as revealed in his diary are certainly unattractive — he could be vindictive, gluttonous, selfish, idle and over-critical of others. He was not a deeply religious man in the sense that the Victorian revivalist clergymen were. But these are at any rate very human failings, in a man doing his job no worse and perhaps rather better than most of his contemporaries.

It is the other and more often expressed side of Parson Woodforde that shines out of the pages of his diary — kindliness, humour salted with irony, friendliness, open-handed generosity to rich and needy poor alike, a direct and unaffected humanity and interest in everything going on around him. He was a welcome guest in all the villages round Weston Longville: Hockering, where Mrs Howes sought his advice on making her Will; East Tuddenham, where he brought a cucumber in his pocket for his ageing but sprightly friend Mr Du Quesne; Mattishall, where the diarist enjoyed a syllabub while playing at quadrille with his host Mr Smith (he

lost 6d); Honingham with Mr and Mrs Townshend, who
'behaved very genteel to us', but whose dinner of eighteen
dishes was spoiled 'by being so frenchified in dressing';
Witchingham, where the self-important Mr and Mrs Jeanes
held sway; Sparham with its beautiful church, where sporty Mr
Stoughton came with dog and gun to lighten the depression of
Woodforde's last years when many of his former friendships
had gone astray.

All these places and their houses and rectories can be
covered in an easy morning's motoring; but only on Shanks'
Pony can the countryside be properly appreciated. So we will
take a walk at Parson Woodforde's stirrup-side to Lyng, where
he rode from time to time to call on Mr Baldwin the Vicar, his
two daughters, Miss Vertue and Miss Nancy, and his bearded
wife, Frances.

*   *   *

The Church of All Saints at Weston Longville was presented
by King Henry VI to New College, Oxford, in whose gift it still
remains. It stands squarely by the road through the village, a
flint and stone fourteenth-century building with a tower about
one hundred years older, approached by a flagged path
through the graveyard.

The massive wooden door opens into a cool, quiet interior
where it is easy to picture Parson Woodforde baptising,
marrying, churching and burying members of his small flock
under the benevolent eye of Squire Custance, whose great
box-pew stands against the south wall. The other pews, 1850
replacements for the earlier boxes, have carved poppy-head
ends and carry beautifully worked hassocks.

On the wall of the north aisle is a superb late fourteenth-
century wall painting of Christ's family tree, the Tree of Jesse,
which features three central panels depicting a very tenderly
enfolded Virgin and Child, a King in Glory and a rapt harpist
supposed to be King David. Various lively figures disport
themselves among the branches, one of them a near-naked
seer pointing a backslider towards salvation. The steps of the
font incorporate a much-eroded Saxon Calvary of Christ with
arms outstretched and head slumped sideways. Under the

lectern mat is a Tudor brass of '*Elyzabeth, late the wyfe of ffyrmyn Rokewood, Esquer*' who died in 1533. She lies near the rood screen, whose lower panels show the twelve Apostles, St John pale-faced and angelic, Judas holding a lance, Simon a carp or pike (Woodforde would have approved of that), and St Peter inspecting his troops from the end of the row with a rather cynical expression.

On the north wall of the chancel is Parson Woodforde's memorial, erected by nephew Bill and niece Nancy, here formally named 'Anna Maria'. It records that '*His Parifhioners held him in the highest esteem and veneration and as a tribute to his memory followed him to the Grave. The poor feel a severe loss as they were the constant objects of his bounty.*'

From the Five Ringers pub, you take the Honingham road past the recently closed red brick school and a row of council houses named Woodforde Close. After a quarter of a mile turn right into a lane (110155) just before the vast and strong-smelling turkey farm that stands on the site of a wartime airfield where the flaming tyres of USAF Liberators burned rubber smears into the runways. Beneath the turkey sheds and half-buried strips of derelict runway lies Hungate Lodge, where Parson Woodforde often walked to visit Mr and Mrs Carbould. They arrived there as newlyweds in February 1794 after the Custances' move to Bath had depressed the parson, and became friends of his. On his first visit on Monday, 10th February 1794, he was 'treated with Chocolate & Wedding Cake', and was soon going to 'Coffee and Tea, by appointment'; also to 'a very genteel Dinner — First Course at the upper End, stewed Tench, Veal Soup, best part of a Rump of Beef boiled, 2 rost Chicken and a Ham, Harrico Mutton, Custard Puddings, backed Mutton Pies, Mashed Potatoes in 3 Scallop Shells brown'd over, Roots 2. Dishes. Second Course. At the upper End, Rabbitts fricasseed, at the lower End Couple of Ducks rosted, Trifle in the Middle, blamange, Cheesecakes, Maccaroni, and small Rasberry-Tartlets. Desert of Fruit mostly that sent by me to them, Peaches, Nectarines and three kinds of Plumbs.' Ten people sat down to this feast: one hopes the guests were suitably impressed, though Mrs Jeanes of Witchingham was pretty sharp with Nancy.

Along the narrow lane where smugglers brought tubs of gin to the kitchen door of the Parsonage is Glebe Farm, on the site of the glebe lands belonging to the Parsonage. Most clergymen of the day let all their glebe lands to local farmers, but most of Woodforde's were farmed for him by faithful Ben Leggatt from Ringland, who entered his service as a young man and remained with him to the end. The lane enters a tunnel of shady trees and passes the gates of the Parsonage (105155).

The building in which Parson Woodforde lived was pulled down in 1840, and the present Old Rectory, a large, handsome red-brick house, stands just beside the site of the original structure. Lyng Old Mill House, which is visited later in the walk, is said to bear a very close resemblance to Woodforde's Parsonage. The Old Rectory garden is a tranquil place of bird-song and soughing wind in the trees, among which still lies the parson's great pond where he killed a hundred toads in one morning, sailed a model ship and netted a seven-pound pike, 'prodigious nice indeed'. Perhaps the copper beech by the present house was known to Will Coleman in his demoted post of gardener, but the stye where Woodforde's '2 Piggs' got

The Old Rectory, Weston Longville. Woodforde's parsonage stood on the left of the present building.

drunk on beer grounds, and the rows of beans and peas set by the parson have long since vanished. Nevertheless, a steady trickle of Woodforde pilgrims turns up each year to ask the owner's permission to gaze at the pond, the trees and the empty lawn where the old Parsonage stood. Then they leave as quietly as they came, down the drive where Farmer Forster staggered after Woodforde's Tithe Audit of 3rd December 1782, having made a thorough nuisance of himself after a skinful of the parson's home-brew.

Leaving the Old Rectory gates, continue along the lane. The fields on the other side contained a number of houses in Woodforde's day which made up the main village of Weston Longville. In a quarter of a mile leave the lane on the right between a red-brick shed and its neighbouring house (102157) and take the footpath, rather boggy in wet weather, that follows behind the house along the edge of the field. When the hedge ends, so does the visible footpath — but steer boldly straight ahead to the road. Most paths across fields hereabouts have fallen victim to the recent hedgeless, big-field farming policy. Squire Custance might have approved of the trend, though: he was one of the few landowners to resist the almost universal enclosure measure of the eighteenth century. However, present-day local farmers have agreed to accept careful walkers' rights to follow the official routes through standing crops — but do keep in single file!

On reaching the road (095158) turn right for one hundred yards, then left along the hedge above the farm buildings, and on with a copse on your right and Collens Green Farm ahead on the crest of a slope. The breeze, the birds and the belching cows are the only sounds to be heard. When the hedge ends, keep steadily on to Hase's Lane (081166) where a signpost directs you along the road towards Lyng.

From this lane there are long views over gently rolling countryside, Lyng lying below and the tree-girt tower of Sparham Church above; a view that might be straight out of a Constable painting. Along this road on 19th November 1790 came running young Barber, the mason's lad, bewailing his folly at enlisting that afternoon at Lyng Fair. A recruiting party was soon hot on his heels with fife and drum; they passed the Parsonage at Weston the following day, but whether they caught up with the wretched youth or not the parson does not tell. The white frontage of Lyng Vicarage (072177) in the valley below attracts the eye, as it must have done for Parson Woodforde, shaking up his horse into a trot with thoughts of dinner and good company.

Directly opposite the Vicarage, a footpath fingerpost directs you downhill through the crops. Make a bee-line for the tower of Sparham Church, bearing to the left of a line of conifers to cross an old stile and reach the road to the left of the house at the crossroads. Lyng lies straight ahead. At the road junction in the village, by a handsome cast-iron sign with a silhouette of the bridge, turn left and then first right to reach Mr Baldwin's Church of St Margaret.

The graveyard grass is mown by an evil-eyed goat, who leaps out at intruders from among the gravestones like Magwitch in *Great Expectations*. Once past this guardian, the Perpendicular flint church is entered through a heavily carved door. The chancel is not aligned centrally with the nave, being on the right-hand side; the story goes that this symbolized the averted head of the crucified Christ, but it may have more to do with inexpert local medieval architects! On the right of the altar is a memorial tablet to Mr Baldwin, his wife and their eleven children — only three survived into their teens, the oldest dying as a midshipman and being buried at Gibraltar, and the Misses Vertue and Nancy departing this life at the tender age of sixteen. The tablet on the left of the altar is to Mr Hamerton, who owned the paper mill at the edge of the village and did Parson Woodforde a number of good turns. Most of the pews carry iron plaques stamped '*Free*', a reminder of the days when the well-off paid for their seats in church; a half-size pew at the back is marked '*Aged Poor*'.

Retrace your steps to the village green and continue along the main road. On the right are the gates of Lyng Vicarage, once the home of Mr Baldwin and scene of many a dinner party enjoyed by Woodforde. Now a private house, it is a large square building, approached by a bridge, dated 1827, over the moat which once completely surrounded the house, and which was rowed by generations of Lyng vicars' children, one of whom still lives close by. In the nineteenth century two bow fronts were added, but otherwise it is largely the same place

*Lyng Mill House, said to bear a close resemblance to the
Weston Parsonage that Woodforde knew*

that Parson Woodforde knew when he rode here with his
friend Mr Du Quesne. The stables where he left his horse still
stand, as does the tithe barn where Mr Baldwin stored the
produce of his glebe lands, though nowadays it is the
nesting-place of wrens and flycatchers. Magnificent trees
surround the house, and the view from the front lawn
overlooks the meadows that lie below Collens Green.

A little further along the road on the left-hand side stands
the old mill house. The paper mill buildings have gone, but the
house makes a charming picture with its own bridge over the
mill-stream just above the main road bridge over the river
Wensum. If it is, as has been suggested, a near replica of
Weston Parsonage, one wonders how all those servants,
relations, friends and drunken farmers crammed into such a
compact building. Parson Woodforde was friendly with the
owner, Mr Hamerton, who managed to get the parson's
wayward nephew Bill into the navy, though later giving his
opinion of Bill as an 'unsteady man' when Bill missed his ship

and returned to Norfolk unrepentant. Woodforde bought 10 quires of paper here for five shillings, and he and Mr Du Quesne marvelled over the mill's machinery. Legend says that the mill is still heard working on certain nights.

Two hundred yards up the road you pass a gate on the right and take the next lane (073179), which leads to the Sparham Pools Nature Reserve. The path skirts the edges of flooded sand-pits, where gorse-smothered islets ring with the quacking and honking of wild fowl. Walkers with field glasses will linger a happy hour here.

With the Wensum gleaming ahead, the path leaves the Nature Reserve and runs between a fence and a hedge whose flinty banks are pock-marked with rabbit scrapes. On either hand are large stands of conifers, and ahead the yellow heaps of sand from present-day excavations. You carry on through a gate and along a hedge, cross a dank ditch and a stile (083182), and walk on a marshy track that winds in and out of the trees with the placid Wensum curving between wooded banks on your right. Soon you turn right on the gravelled track to Walsis' Farm below Walsis' Hill, a terraced and sheep-shaven rabbit warren. At the farm the track becomes a concrete road, which is followed to a big barn (092183) at the corner of a copse. Here you bear right past the barn, over a gate and diagonally across Lenwade Cricket Ground to a gate that gives access to the grounds of the imposing, black-and-white timbered Lenwade House Hotel. Cross the drive and continue down a narrow path between fence and trees as far as the sunken football field. To avoid the Lenwade Trout Fisheries' private land beside the river, a detour must be made along the main Fakenham Road, turning right again at the Post Office down Lenwade Street, which curves left and rejoins the main road a quarter of a mile further on. In Lenwade Street are two good examples of flint building side by side — number 11 of cut blocks, and number 15 (whatever happened to unlucky number 13?) of flint pebbles — as well as a fine Methodist chapel and, on the corner of Fakenham Road, a striking old house with arched windows and door that Woodforde would have known.

As you leave Lenwade Street, three major Woodforde sites lie ahead — the altered and enlarged mill with its apple trees and ornamental garden where the Parson bought flour from

Miller Foster; the Bridge Inn where, at the end of their occasional visits, his sisters Pounsett and Clarke would catch the Lenwade Chaise to Norwich on their long journey back to Somerset; and Lenwade Bridge. The original three-arched stone bridge was replaced in 1927 by a structure of five concrete arches; but unlike Henry Williamson's Rothern Bridge, nothing remains here of the bridge where, on 21st May 1778, Woodforde caught 'a Prodigious fine Pike which weighed 8 Pound and half and it had in his Belly another Pike, of above a Pound'.

On another occasion in 1781 he caught a pike between Lenwade Bridge and Morton which was a yard long and weighed more than thirteen pounds. The next day 'I gave my Company for dinner my great Pike which was rosted and a Pudding in his Belly', laid on two of the parson's largest dishes on top of the kitchen window shutters. 'I never saw a nobler Fish at any table, it was very well cooked, and tho' so large was declared by all the Company to be prodigious fine eating, being so moist.'

If you arrive at the Bridge Inn during opening hours, you can see in the bar a photograph of the old bridge, and also one of Squire Custance's Weston House, the last item of Woodforde interest on the walk. The photograph shows an imposing, square mansion, handsomely pillared, porticoed and balconied, with the stables just visible behind. To reach the gates of Weston House, cross the bridge and take the road to the right signposted 'Hockering 4, Mattishall 6'. A quarter of a mile down the road are the spear-blade gates on wrought-iron pillars and the grey stone lodge of Weston House (104182), which the Squire had built and moved into on 2nd August 1781. Many a day Parson Woodforde rode through the grounds to the house, sometimes to dinner, sometimes to tea, sometimes just for an hour's chat with whoever happened to be at home. When Mr and Mrs Custance were out, the parson might 'stay about an Hour with the little Folks'. If niece Nancy was included in the invitation the Squire would send his carriage to spare her the rough ride, in marked contrast to the high and mighty Jeaneses at Witchingham. Apart from his own beloved Parsonage, these acres of peaceful parkland probably saw Parson Woodforde's happiest hours.

The estate was sold in the 1920s, the last Custance to live there being Olive, wife of Lord Alfred Douglas of Oscar Wilde notoriety. The house was pulled down and the stables converted into living quarters by the new owner, a Lancashire mill owner by the name of Charles Clutsom, whose memorial tablet is in Weston Church.

On the other side of the road from Weston House gates you can see Weston Old Hall (102178), whose gates are a quarter of a mile further on. The Custances never lived there, but cannibalized it for the building of their new house. The road continues between high hedges to a turning on the left signposted '*Weston Longville*' (101172). Take this road and walk past the red-tiled roof of Dairy Farm to an unmarked turning opposite Upper Farm (109167). On the left, a few yards along this lane, are the back gates to Squire Custance's park, which the parson used as a short cut on his rides from Weston by the Squire's kind invitation. Beyond the gate is a grand old twisted oak tree past which Woodforde clopped up the drive through broad grassy parkland to the House.

Returning to the road at Upper Farm, a long straight stretch brings you back to the church at Weston Longville where Parson Woodforde preached, and where his bones are laid to rest.

The Parson Woodforde Society
c/o The Secretary, 76 Spencer Street, Norwich, Norfolk.
Founded in 1968 with two aims — to extend and develop members' knowledge of James Woodforde's life and the society in which he lived, and to provide an opportunity for members who are linked by a common interest in the diaries to meet once a year at a place associated with the diarist — usually in alternate years in Somerset and Norfolk.
The Society publishes an excellent quarterly Journal.

Local Library
Central Library, Bethel Street, Norwich, Norfolk NR2 1NJ

With Tom Brown, Harry East and the Tadpole on the Barby Run

Tom Brown's Schooldays by Thomas Hughes
First published by Macmillan, 1867
Penguin paperback, 1971

(Rugby School — Whitehall Recreation Ground — Great Central Railway — Onley Lane — Barby Hill — Rains Brook — Dunchurch Road — Rugby School. About eight miles by road, disused railway and field paths. Easy walking, though the way is not always obvious on the ground; hedges and fences delineate the route.)

O.S.– 1:50,000 Sheet No. 140 'Leicester & Coventry'
1:25,000 Sheet No. SP 47/57 'Rugby'

On the lawn outside the library of Rugby School stands a tall white statue of a balding side-whiskered Victorian gentleman, looking out across the Barby Road to the wide green expanse of the Close. His gaze encompasses the H-shaped rugby football posts set into the hallowed turf, the encircling trees, the mellow brick walls that surround the Close, and beyond them the turrets and towers of the School House, where he spent the eight years that, recounted in a school story twenty years later, made his name a household word throughout Britain, her Empire and former colonies. The book was *Tom Brown's Schooldays* and its author, Thomas Hughes, the subject of the statue. Though nowadays remembered chiefly for his masterpiece of evocative writing, Tom Hughes was a remarkable man even by the standards of his age, which produced so many outstanding public figures. As author, politician, athlete, lawyer, church reformer, champion of labour and zealous Christian Socialist, he was one of the most

Opposite: *Thomas Hughes, a portrait from Rugby School*

influential men in England in the middle of the nineteenth century. Yet he achieved all this with no special intellectual equipment or oratorical brilliance, remaining always a simple, direct and humble man, dedicated to hitting hard and straight at the numerous injustices and hypocrisies that roused his gladiatorial spirit. 'The Browns are a fighting family,' he wrote of Tom Brown's kin; 'about their fight there can be no question. Wherever hard knocks of any kind, visible or invisible, are going, there the Brown who is nearest must shove in his carcass.' Tom Hughes spent his whole life, fortune and energy shoving in his carcass among the hard knocks.

He was born on 20th October 1822 in the village of Uffington in the Vale of the White Horse in Berkshire, the son of a scholarly gentleman of leisure. His early childhood was of the outdoor kind recounted in *Tom Brown's Schooldays* — playing football and cricket with the village children, wrestling, fishing, and walking and riding around his beloved Vale. In 1833, after a spell at a private school near Winchester, his father sent him away to public school at Rugby, then an out-of-the-way Warwickshire market town. This was a decision not lightly taken in those days. Public schools had none of the social cachet that makes them so keenly sought after by rich parents nowadays. They were seen as sinks of iniquity where boys were given every opportunity to learn bad habits and idleness, presided over by faded classical scholars whose job was simply to keep order in their huge, almost unmanageable classes. Vicious bullying, gambling, drinking and neglect were the order of the day. At Rugby there was a state of open warfare between the boys of the school and the local farmers, whose crops were trampled, fences broken and poultry stolen by the 'young gentlemen' as a matter of course. The younger boys endured savage beatings from their seniors, long hours of fagging (often being set pointless tasks for the sadistic pleasure of their superiors) and bad teaching. Their only consolation was the knowledge that they would one day wield similar power over the next wretched generation of fags.

However, Rugby was lucky in its Headmaster, the brilliant and unswervingly high-principled Dr Thomas Arnold, who had come to the school in 1828 determined to lift it from its intellectual and moral trough. Arnold in his reign of fourteen years succeeded in raising the standards of teaching and communal life to such a height that Rugby came to be taken as the model of an English public school — a triumph which gained further impetus when his pupil's famous book came out in 1857. Arnold was an ardent Christian who believed in the potential of each individual boy to respond to the Christian message and to shoulder responsibility for himself and for others. By the excellence of his classroom teaching, his high expectations of the boys, his firm discipline (not sparing the rod) and his moving sermons, Arnold forged a new kind of public school. Tom Hughes was won over by this charismatic man, and never lost his admiration for him as a great teacher and influence for Christian morality in a corrupt and degraded system. Under Arnold, he became open-minded and felt the first stirrings of the Socialist principles that were later to make him the champion of the post-Industrial Revolution workers with their many grievances. 'I passed all those years under the spell of this place and of Arnold,' he wrote in 1891 of his time at Rugby, 'and for half a century have never ceased to thank God for it.'

Tom Hughes did well at Rugby. Though never one of Arnold's favoured circle of clever boys, he excelled at sports, becoming Captain of the Cricket XI and of Big-side football — this was nearly twenty years after William Webb Ellis 'with a fine disregard for the rules of football as played in his time first took the ball in his arms and ran with it'.

In 1842, the year of Arnold's death, Hughes went up to Oxford University. At Oriel College he kept up his sporting interests and after a slow start put in enough work to gain his degree in 1845. He trained as a barrister, living in Lincoln's Inn and coming into contact with the gin shops, brothels and slums of Dickensian London — experiences which confirmed him in his Socialism. At Oxford he had turned from the Toryism of his upbringing to Liberalism, finding himself in agreement with the newly organized Chartist movement and its demand for universal suffrage. Now he was introduced to Christian Socialism, a fusion of Socialist principles under the banner of Christian belief which became the guiding light of his life. He spoke at workers' meetings, taught at workers' education classes, wrote pamphlets, raised money, and helped to form trades associations whose purpose was to enable workers to own and manage their own places of work and to share the profits. 'We were young, saucy, and so thoroughly convinced that we were right, that we cared, shall I say, not a d — n,' Hughes wrote of his and his friends' activities.

In 1847 he married Fanny Ford, a happy union which supported and strengthened him for the rest of his life. In 1848 he was called to the Bar, but continued to spend all his free time working for the emerging co-operative movement. He dashed up and down the country on the newly opened railways, exhorting and encouraging the ever-growing trades unions. The Christian Socialist movement was soon pushed aside by the materially minded workers' leaders, and its trades associations became bankrupt one after the other; but Hughes ploughed on, helping to found the Working Men's College where he taught, argued and boxed with any and everyone.

By 1856 he had begun to try his hand at writing, mostly light verse and hearty accounts of his travelling in the cause of Christian Socialism. In that year, however, he sat down to write the book that brought together all his most powerful assets — vitality, humour, religious conviction, directness and ability to grip and move his public. When *Tom Brown's Schooldays* was published by Macmillan on 24th April 1857, it was an instant success. In its first seven months it sold out of five editions, brought Hughes more than £1,000 in royalties and made his name.

Few school stories had been written before Hughes's book, and none had possessed anything like its accuracy, power or depth. Under the thin disguise of honest, manly Tom Brown, Hughes wrote of his own experiences at Rugby, his love for the School and its Headmaster, and the effect of a shining light in the dark. He cheerfully admitted that his intention was to preach, and preach he did; yet with such careful balance that the story flows from one escapade to the next unimpeded by the moral lessons drawn from each incident. It is a superbly remembered and presented boy's-eye view of life — a remarkable achievement by a man of thirty-five, but testimony to the influence of Hughes's boyhood on his adult perceptions.

The reader follows Tom Brown from his idyllic childhood in the Vale of the White Horse to Arnold's Rugby, rough, in many ways barbaric, just beginning to be altered by the Doctor's example. There are many threads that run through the book — the gradual change from the roastings, lickings and other cruelties of Tom's early schooldays through the 'War of Independence' to the benign regime of his own school captaincy: the vivid and utterly realistic accounts of schoolboy scrapes from illicit poaching expeditions to bird-nesting, fighting and 'cribbing' lessons; famous accounts of the Rugby football game on the day of Tom's arrival, and the cricket match on his last day at Rugby. Hughes's greatest achievement, however, is the life he breathes into the characters that hold the stage: the gross, cowardly bully Flashman; quizzical, happy-go-lucky Harry East, Tom's best friend; the patriarchal school hero old Brooke; the kindly eccentric Diggs, and the even more eccentric naturalist Martin; frail little Arthur whom Tom befriends and who comes to exert as much influence on our hero as Dr Arnold himself. The Doctor only comes to centre stage occasionally, as a kindly father-figure, a clarion call in Chapel, the grim wielder of the birch; but it is his teaching, filtered down to Tom through his experiences and the lessons he learns from them, which turns the feckless boy through trial and error into a young man with a mission to a sinful world. Hughes undoubtedly played down Arnold's tendency to force-feed the brightest boys with intellectual and spiritual material that only a few of them could handle, and his overcensoriousness of harmless pranks; but he leaves the reader with a clear picture of a man admired and revered by all who came under his rule.

Hughes's hobby-horses — his nostalgia for the Merrie England of the benevolent squire and the deserving peasant who knows his place, for example — appear to modern minds to lie uneasily with the egalitarian philosophy of Christian Socialism. But the main message of the book — honest service in the cause of good — struck home with its readers then as now, brought Tom Hughes's name to the attention of the public at large, and kept it there.

In 1859 Hughes and his wife moved from their home in Wimbledon to Mayfair, where he indulged his love of entertaining and being entertained. He was never happier than at a country-house weekend, rod in hand and cigar in mouth. These leanings towards the Establishment began to colour his attitudes to the cause of labour, and led him to back conservative trade union leaders who were opposed to strikes and favoured arbitration. In this cause he spent himself tirelessly, and became increasingly involved in strengthening links between England and America, relations between the two countries being at a very low ebb after the skirmishes of recent years. He supported the anti-slavery, pro-North side in the Civil War, and urged disaffected English workers to emigrate and start a new life in the New World. Hughes's dream was to have an alliance of English-speaking nations as the leaders and arbitrators of the world's affairs.

His subsequent books never recaptured the power of *Tom Brown's Schooldays*. *The Scouring of the White Horse* (1858) was a wordy flop, *Tom Brown at Oxford* (1861) a shadow of its famous predecessor. Hughes suffered the same problem as many other creative artists before and since — he had reached his zenith with his first work, and all was downhill from then on. In public life, however, he was still a force to be reckoned with. In July 1865 he was elected Liberal MP for Lambeth, and served that constituency for three years; though his electors quickly became disillusioned with his Parliamentary performance. He backed the ill-fated Liberal Reform Bill with its demands for greater democracy, and helped set up businesses on a co-operative sharing basis with his own money; but he did not spend enough time on the interests of the publicans and traders of Lambeth. In 1868 he switched seats and was returned by the Somerset market town of Frome, but again expended his energies on the co-operative movement rather than on the affairs of his constituents. His strong Christian principles set him at odds with many of the trades union leaders; he found them strident and antagonistic to the established Church, and they found him not radical enough for their purposes. He was beginning to be a figure of fun in the House of Commons; hard-nosed career politicians inevitably cast him in the role of an overgrown, idealistic Tom Brown, tilting ineffectually at windmills. He was in fact losing his grip on the pulse of the workers' movements. He attacked labour for its greed and self-interest, and bitterly resented the new socialist indifference to Christian ideals. Perhaps mercifully, his attempt in 1874 to switch seats again to Marylebone failed dismally; he was not even adopted as the Liberal candidate. Not without regrets, and with one further challenge at Salisbury, he was forced to admit that his days in Parliament were over.

Now Hughes poured his energy and money into a far-fetched scheme to establish a colony for public schoolboys in America, where by the sweat of their brows they could build a new Jerusalem and set an example of selfless service to the world. In 1870 he had made a highly successful trip to America, which had confirmed his sympathetic feelings for that country. In 1879 he associated himself with a group of like-minded rich men who formed the Board of Aid to Land Ownership and purchased 7,000 acres of rough land on the Cumberland plateau of Tennessee for £150,000 — a bad omen, as they were roundly swindled by the American agent and paid three times the actual worth of the site. The new town of Rugby was planned, farms laid out and manufacturing businesses set up, and the first ship-loads of Tom Browns made their way out to the swamps, forests, and barren uplands. In August 1880, Hughes went to Tennessee to meet for himself 'a set of as stalwart good fellows as ever sang a chorus or ate a beef-steak at midnight'. He was delighted with the settlement, and returned to England in high hopes.

Cracks soon began to appear in the unlikely edifice, however. Upper-class English families jumped at this golden opportunity to send their black sheep to the other side of the world, and the 'stalwart good fellows' were soon intermingled with idlers and no-hopers. The land was bad, and there was an outbreak of typhoid in 1881 which claimed 17 lives. The colony's own magazine, the *Rugbeian*, claimed: 'Truly a very ridiculous mouse have these Cumberland mountains brought forth.'

A fresh injection of capital in 1882 eased matters for a few years. In 1885 the Arnold School was opened, and a few more brickworks and canning plants started; but the end of the dream was not far off. Hughes's own son George came to look Rugby over and wisely decided not to stay. After painfully long-drawn-out death throes, the Board of Aid sold out in 1891 and Hughes was left to lick his wounds. Ten years earlier he

had written: 'I have risked in it more than I should have done
. . . and have sorely repented it.' When all the accounts had
been added, Hughes was £7,000 the poorer, though
undoubtedly wiser.

His wife, Fanny, was a great comfort to him at this time of
broken hopes as he struggled to salvage some self-respect from
his string of failures. In 1882 he had become a County Court
judge, and moved to Chester, where he subsided into a mellow
old age. He still 'shoved in his carcass' for a few more hard
knocks, losing many old friends by his opposition to Home
Rule for Ireland and continuing to champion the cause of
labour while becoming more and more suspicious of its
leaders. In spite of rheumatism and gout, his athletic younger
days paid dividends in a healthy old age until he died in
Brighton on 22nd March 1896, on his way to Italy. Of the small
fortune that Tom Brown had brought him, he left only £8,412,
having spent the rest in a typically open-handed fashion on his
various philanthropic schemes.

Tom Brown's Schooldays ran to seventy editions in
Hughes's lifetime, and remains his major literary
achievement, though his *Manliness of Christ*, a collection of his
lectures to the Working Men's College, was a simple and direct
statement of his faith which found favour with critics and
public when it was published in 1879. The Labour movement
has long since forgotten its hot-headed, faithful champion,
Tom Hughes, with his warmth, honesty and determination to
find and promote the good in all men and situations. He stated
his own principles with characteristic simplicity in *Tom
Brown's Schooldays*: 'If you do fight, fight it out; and don't
give in while you can stand and see.'

*　*　*

Anyone setting out to retrace the course of the Barby Run as
described in Chapter VII of *Tom Brown's Schooldays* is in for
a game of guesswork. The main problem is that, while
Hughes's description is very precise as to the number of fields
crossed and their geographical positions, he seems to have
amalgamated two set runs into one — the Barby Hill Run and
the Barby Village Run. Both are minutely laid out in a book of

Rugby School runs, published in 1902, but neither corresponds exactly to Hughes's descriptions. Tom Brown and his friends got thoroughly lost, which further complicates the issue, as do the changes that have taken place since 1834 in field boundaries, and the rise and fall in relative importance of local roads and lanes.

Hughes says that the 'hares' were 'generally viewed on the side of Barby Hill' and that 'everyone who comes in within a quarter of an hour of the hares'll be counted, if he has been round Barby Church.' Yet the Barby Run as described in the 1902 book turns for home a good mile and a half short of Barby Church. Tom and his friends had certainly not reached Barby when they were directed into the short cut back to Rugby by young Brooke, who then 'steams away for the run-in', not towards Barby. Harry East tells the Doctor proudly after the run that 'we got round Barby all right', but the story does not bear out his claim. Perhaps East was allowing himself a little extra glory to keep up his spirits as he stood before the dreaded Doctor covered in mud from head to toe.

The run officially ended at the Cock Robin public house on the Dunchurch—Rugby road, where, as the Tadpole remarked before their attempt: 'if a fellow gets in at the end, Big-side stands ale and bread and cheese, and a bowl of punch; and the Cock's such a famous place for ale.' This treat was probably laid on for those hardy enough to add the extra two and a half miles round Barby Church to their task.

This walk, therefore, tries to kill all birds with one stone by following the 1902 Barby Hill Run to its turning-point east of Barby, and then attempting to follow the never-ending lane which so tried the endurance of Tom Brown, Harry East and the Tadpole.

Big-side 'hare and hounds' cross-country runs took place in late winter on Fridays. On Thursday all fags were required to find and tear up paper for 'scent'. The wise locked away their school books until the run was under way — no books were sacrosanct. Rugby School legend has it that the entire library of Henry Holyoake, Headmaster from 1687–1731, was discovered in a cellar by eager fags and torn up for 'scent'.

On the Friday, fifty or sixty School House boys would set off from the main School House gates, facing the top of the High Street, where our walk begins (502750). These gates give onto the quad which is surrounded by the tiny, cell-like studies of the boys, virtually unchanged since Tom Hughes's day. Turn left to pass the entrance to the Headmaster's house, and continue over a set of traffic lights along Hillmorton Road, keeping on the right-hand pavement. On the opposite side, at the corner of Church Walk, is the birthplace of the poet Rupert Brooke. At the next set of traffic lights (508748) Whitehall Road on the left leads up to a crossroads where the 'old gable-ended house' of White Hall marked the official start of the run — it was pulled down in 1870. Here the 'hares' — Hughes himself was one of these fleet-footed running specialists — buckled onto their belts the canvas bags of 'scent', embroidered in red with '*Big-side Bags*'. Two of these bags are preserved in the School Library's Museum. The hares then set off across open fields, followed six minutes later by the 'hounds' on the trail of the paper scent which the hares threw out as they ran.

From the traffic lights on Hillmorton Road, turn right at the War Memorial into the Whitehall Recreation Ground, and head diagonally across the grass to a path at the bottom left-hand corner. You pass a big modern sports centre, and where the road bends left continue on the footbridge over Sow Brook (508743), five fields and five trampled hedges from the start of the run in Hughes's day. On the far bank turn left along a path which leads to Trevor White Drive, where you turn right into Pytchley Road. Follow the road to the bridge over a great cutting (515739) through which the trains of the Great Central Railway once thundered on their way from London to Nottingham. Hughes never knew this magnificent white elephant of a railway, which was opened in 1899 as a direct London—Midlands route, and closed southwards from Rugby in 1966 and northwards in 1969. All the lessons learned in railway engineering over the previous half-century were applied in the building of the Great Central — wide, straight, superbly engineered track; expresses that gobbled up the miles imperiously; well-planned and frequent services. The trouble was that the whole enterprise came into being fifty years too late, and in the last analysis was an unnecessary duplication of the already adequate railway routes.

Do not cross the railway by the bridge, but turn right through railings and walk along the top of the cutting. The rugby football pitches on your right behind the trees are known as 'Far Polo' — they were laid out on old polo fields, whose red-brick stables can be seen in the distance. Just before the bridge that carries the B4429 road across the railway (515732), scramble down the cutting-side onto the track, and walk on. This section of the old railway line is now a nature reserve, sometimes disturbed by motor-bike riders — so look out! Where the cutting-side becomes shallow, there is a good view over to the left towards Barby Hill, whose clumps of trees and squares of fields form the main feature in a rather featureless landscape. The Malvern Hills can be seen from the top of Barby Hill on a clear day. Tom Brown and his companions ran in the fields to the left, down the slopes of the ground towards Rains Brook in the valley bottom. The ploughed fields soon sorted out the men from the boys, as 'An Old Rugbeian' noted in his book *Recollections of Rugby* (1848).

> 'The first good stiff piece of ploughed land reduced the number to one half; and the second or third found very few besides the regular set, amounting to about eight or ten . . .'

Tom Hughes also remembered the falling-out of the faint-hearted:

> 'In the second or third field the tailing off began, and all but the cracks fell out by twos or threes, the studious to get back to their studies, and the rest of us to go "pecking" (throwing stones at birds) along the hedgerows, or to strike the road and patter along it to Bilton, Brownsover, Newhold, or wherever the run in might be.'

Crafty hounds began to edge away to the right and so shorten their run-in, but gallant Tom and his friends were still trying to keep up with young Brooke — 'they struggle after him, sobbing and plunging along, Tom and East pretty close, and Tadpole, whose big head begins to pull him down, some thirty yards behind.'

At a broken bridge (516725) the line of the old railway is crossed by Onley Lane, 'the most trist and least frequented of any road out of Rugby' according to Matthew Holbeche

Bloxam, a near contemporary of Hughes.

Turn left down the lane, passing great oblong heaps of spoil, dug from the cutting by the navvies nearly a hundred years ago and dumped in the fields on your right, and cross Rains Brook by a bridge (520720). Local legend says that between Rains Brook and Barby Wood 'a fierce battle is to be fought one of these days; three kings are to be present, and a miller with two thumbs on one hand is to hold their horses. Rains Brook, this petty stream, is to flow with blood.' It was in this brook that the Tadpole (later to become in real life Headmaster of Marlborough School) came to grief in the 'stiff clay banks'. However, Tom and East had 'too little run left in themselves to pull up for their own brothers', and staggered on for another three fields before young Brooke took pity on them. The lane he directed them to might well be Onley Lane, were it not for his assurance that they would 'hit the Dunchurch Road below the Cock'. The only lane which fits this description has long since declined to a grassy track by the hedges, but it can be found by following Onley Lane over the M45 and the Oxford Canal (opened on New Year's Day 1790, and therefore in existence in Hughes's day, but strangely not mentioned in his account) and turning right where Onley Lane bends sharply to the left at the top of the next rise (526709).

After a few hundred yards, go over barbed wire on your right, and re-cross the Oxford Canal by a red-brick hump-back bridge (522709). Make for the bottom left-hand corner of the next field, and cross the Great Central Railway by the gap of a broken bridge. On the far side bear left to cross a gate in the top left-hand corner of the field, and carry on with the fence and hedge on your left. This was once the course of the winding lane which led by tortuous twists and turns to Rugby, and must have seen many a dreary slog back to school by exhausted young hounds left behind by the hue and cry. The monotonous landscape is not improved by the low grey bulk of Onley Under-25 prison away to the left beyond its barbed wire fences.

In a couple of hundred yards keep on the right of the hedge as it forks right at 45° (515709), making for an oak tree with a crown shaped like three feathery fingers. Walk along the hedge round the edge of a large field to cross over the already crumbling bridge over the M45. At the bottom of the ramp bear right through a gap in the hedge, and walk down to the bottom left-hand corner of the next field where the path runs straight on into a thicket of thorny bushes. Once inside the thicket, the wide, flat formation of the old lane can be distinguished more clearly than hitherto.

You cross Rains Brook again, and turn right into an open field. Ahead the ground rises up a slope up which the official footpath continues; but the farmer has directed walkers to keep right along the brook to the fence on the far side of the next field (508714). Here the path follows the fence up the slope on a headland which may be on either side of the fence, depending on the season. If on the left, cross over to the right of the fence by a gate three-quarters of the way up the slope. Somewhere up here the wretched Tadpole rejoined Tom and East, having lost a shoe in the wet clay of Rains Brook. 'The sight of him, notwithstanding, cheered them, for he was some degrees more wretched than they.'

At the top of the rise, just beyond a sunken pond in a dingle, cross the left-hand of two gates set close together and walk up to the B4429 road. Cross it and turn right for a few yards, then left at a public footpath sign into a track which runs towards the tall spire of the Catholic Church of St Marie, dwarfing the dumpy tower of Rugby School Chapel. The track bends to the right, and in a few yards you take a path on the left (502727) which wriggles between new houses, crosses Ecton Leys and comes to a recreation ground. Turn left down the hedge to cross Long Furlong and continue, overshadowed by trees, to the Dunchurch Road. Here Tom and his companions met up with the Pig and Whistle (the Oxford-to-Rugby coach), 'with one lamp lighted, and two spavined horses in the shafts'. They were given a lift for a shilling by 'the old scarecrow of a coachman' and so arrived back at school, unutterably tired, wet and filthy, forty minutes after locking-up time.

Shanks' Pony will carry you on down the hill and up again past the School House Close to reach Hillmorton Road opposite Gilbert's celebrated rugby-ball shop. Turn right past the school gates to the traffic lights, where you turn right again down Barby Road, and right yet again through the Close gates (these may be locked during school holidays) to finish the walk (503749).

Across the grass of the Close came stealing Tom, East and the Tadpole, to pass through the little wooden gate in the wall on the right, trespass across the Doctor's garden, and sneak into the house by the servants' entrance — where they were promptly arrested and sent up with chattering teeth to face the Doctor. On this occasion, their lord and master spared the rod and packed them off to the Housekeeper for cold meat and buttered toast — a cosy ending to the dismal day.

Beyond the little gate a pink granite plaque in the wall celebrates William Webb Ellis's innovative experiment with a football in 1823 — this spot is a place of pilgrimage to rugby players and enthusiasts the world over.

A short walk down the Barby Road from the Close gates brings you to the School Library on the left, where you can pay your respects to Tom Hughes on his pedestal.

Information on Local History and Walking
Rugby Local History Research Group, c/o The Secretary, 1 St John's Avenue, Rugby, Warwicks
Ramblers' Association, Midland Area (Rugby Group), c/o The Secretary, 12 Morson Crescent, Rugby, Warwicks CV21 4AL

Local Library
Rugby Library, St Matthew's Street, Rugby, Warwicks CV21 3BZ

Useful Books
Thomas Hughes — the life of the author of 'Tom Brown's Schooldays' by Edward C. Mack and W.H.G. Armytage. Published by Ernest Benn, 1952
Rugby As It Was by the Rugby Local History Research Group. Published by Hendon Publishing Co. Ltd. 1979 (widely available in Rugby, with many fascinating old photographs)
25 Walks near Rugby compiled by the Rugby Group of the Ramblers' Association. Published 1982

Opposite: *Statue of Thomas Hughes, outside the Temple Reading Room, Rugby School*

Cider with Rosie and Young Laurie Lee

Cider with Rosie by Laurie Lee
First published by the Hogarth Press, 1959
Penguin paperback, 1970

(Laurie's house — Squire Jones's — the pond — Rosie's field — Sixpence Robinson's — Trillgate Farm and Deadcombe Bottom — Bulls Cross and Emmanuel Twinning's — Brith Wood — murder at the War Memorial — Joseph and Hannah Brown's — the church — the school — the Woolpack Inn. About two miles by lanes and tracks, with a climb to a high-level view)

O.S.– 1:50,000 Sheet No. 162 'Gloucester and Forest of Dean'
1:25,000 Sheet No. SO 80 'Stroud'

Laurie Lee came to live in the little Cotswold village of Slad, two miles north-east of Stroud, at the age of three. His mother, Annie, the daughter of a coachman, had left school at thirteen and gone into service like so many other young girls of that Victorian age. She came home to help her father run a pub in the nearby village of Sheepscombe before answering an advertisement for a housekeeper placed by a widower with four young children to look after. Annie, a lively, handsome and scatter-brained woman of thirty, fell in love with her employer and soon married him. Four more children arrived, of whom Laurie was the third. In 1917 Mr Lee left home to join the Army Pay Corps, and made a life for himself away from his family. Annie brought her eight young charges to Slad, to set up home in a cottage at the foot of a bank leading down from the road through the village.

Here Laurie lived with his brothers and sisters, gradually becoming aware of the world outside the familiar walls of the house. He went to school, first in the village and later at

Opposite: *Laurie Lee*

Stroud. Leaving at the age of fifteen, he worked in an office in Stroud until 1934, when he left home to seek his fortune by busking with his fiddle and labouring on building sites in London. In 1935 he went to Spain, returning there during the Civil War to help the anti-Fascist cause. The story of those journeys is told in his books *As I Walked Out One Midsummer Morning* and *A Rose for Winter*.

During the Second World War Laurie Lee worked as Publications Editor for the Ministry of Information, and became involved with film-making. After the war he continued to write poetry, an occupation he had begun in childhood, which was then beginning to make his name and which has now established him as one of Britain's leading poets. However, it was the publication of *Cider with Rosie* which won him a lasting place in the hearts of the general reading public.

Cider with Rosie tells the story of those early years of life in Slad as young Laurie came to know his neighbours and the village hierarchy of squire, vicar, local gentry, farmers, labourers, old folk and young playmates. It is a poet's book, its chapters crammed with vivid recollections. Each person, place and incident is taken out and held before the light of Laurie Lee's descriptive genius, to be fixed in the reader's mind with phrases that often owe more to poetry than prose.

'The scullery was water, where the old pump stood. And it had everything else that was related to water: thick steam of Mondays edgy with starch; soapsuds boiling, bellying and popping, creaking and whispering, rainbowed with light and winking with a million windows. Bubble bubble, toil and grumble, rinsing and slapping of sheets and shirts, and panting Mother rowing her red arms like oars in the steaming waves. Then the linen came up on a stick out of the pot, like pastry, or woven suds, or sheets of moulded snow.'

The whole book is rich in these alliterative, rhythmic passages. To read it is to plunge into a stream of superbly crafted writing which never palls or fails in its purpose of capturing the images that make up a patchwork quilt of a story.

Laurie Lee begins with his house and family, the whole world of a tiny boy, and broadens his scope as his horizons widen to take in neighbours, the village school and some dark and tragic local events. Then we are treated to a masterly, loving and clear-sighted account of his mother, her memories of past glories and her present struggle to keep a large family going in the face of hardship and her own harum-scarum nature. Descriptions follow of life in the village in winter and summer, and of the illnesses and traumas that coloured much of his childhood. His four heroic uncles in turn burst briefly onto the stage, followed by accounts of village celebrations — Peace Day in 1919, outings with the family and the choir, and the classic description of the rag-bag of local talent that made up the Parochial Church Tea and Annual Entertainment. Then comes the chapter from which the book takes its name, in which Laurie Lee charts the burgeoning of sexual awareness, early experiments with village girls and the afternoon of 'cidrous kisses' with Rosie Burdock under a hay wagon.

The book ends with a description of the decay and death of the inward-looking, self-contained village society which had survived almost unchanged for hundreds of years. Motor cars, radio, jobs away from the area, and new ideas and influences combined to wrench open the closed community. The old folk died off, shaken and disturbed by changes they had not foreseen and could not understand, and the youngsters moved away. As the village underwent this metamorphosis, so did Laurie Lee's family, with suitors taking the girls off one by one and the boys, too, breaking free of home and Mother. Laurie Lee was present at one of history's great moments of upheaval, and *Cider with Rosie* is shot through with revelations of its effect on its victims.

It comes as a shock to discover how small is the stage across which so many people and events pass. Slad and its fields and woods occupy only a couple of miles of ground, but Laurie Lee's account is so densely populated that the reader is constantly reminded as he walks and looks around him of characters and incidents from the book. This short walk does not attempt to cover more than a sample of the delights of *Cider with Rosie*, but readers should be able to place for themselves many more favourite scenes from the story as they go.

*   *   *

The house where Annie Lee brought up her eight children is set at the foot of a steep bank below the B4070 road that runs through Slad. Coming up the valley northwards from Stroud you pass the Woolpack Inn on your right and the church above the road on your left, and then come to a side lane on the right that leads off below the level of the main road. The Lees' house, now called Rosebank, crouches snugly in its neatly hedged garden below the head of the lane (873075), a sturdy seventeenth-century building with a dark-grey roof blotched with lichen and moss, warm golden-grey Cotswold stone walls, red-brick chimney stacks and stout stone mullions in the old windows. The front of the house looks out over the Slad Brook in the valley-bottom to fields that slope up to the wooded skyline opposite.

The house had been a small country manor and a pub, but, by the time the Lees moved in, it was divided into three separate cottages. In the other two lived Granny Wallon, or ''Er-Down-Under', with her home-made wines; and Granny Trill, or ''Er-Up-Atop', who lived her own life of snuff-taking and almanac-consulting to her own daily timetable (breakfast at four in the morning, in bed by five in the afternoon), and who took Laurie's sisters down several pegs when they went to show off their finery to her: 'You baggages! You jumped-up varmints! Be off, or I'll fetch me broom!'

Mother Lee coped with her large brood from day to day in their portion of the house, the longer wing of the building. Laurie Lee's book contains a magical evocation of a fire-lit evening in the kitchen, each member of the family going about his or her occupation — giggling, squabbling, swapping local scandal, drawing, murmuring and gradually falling asleep. Later on in the life of the family suitors began to call for the girls, and the boys found their own amusements in the woods and lanes around Slad. The bank that slopes up from the house to the road was the scene of Laurie's first encounters with pretty Jo, the acquiescent partner in games of 'doctor and patient', who was his first but by no means last fellow-traveller into the land of sex-games. Village morality in those days exerted its own checks and balances — public ridicule, 'sending to Coventry' and the like — which made sure that offenders against the unwritten codes of behaviour were controlled without interference from police or other outsiders. When Laurie and Jo were spotted by a couple of cowmen, the voyeurs laughed their heads off and left it at that.

You walk down the lane that branches off from the main road above Rosebank, between new houses designed to fit in with the older buildings but still standing out in the rawness of their unweathered Cotswold stone. Frith Wood strides up the valley on the crest of the ridge above the main road to your left, enclosing the village. It is easy to see how old folk in Laurie Lee's day half-believed that the world ended beyond their valley. The lane rounds a corner and dips downhill between tall sycamores and horse chestnuts. Half-way down, there is a good view over a gate on your right of Steanbridge House (875077), a dignified manor house with tall chimneys on steeply pitched roofs, once the residence of that 'crumbling moot tree' Squire Jones who slept through sermons and quavered through speeches, and whose death brought about the dissolution of his estate, and with it the old village community. Young Laurie, uncomfortably dressed up as John Bull, was given a prize by the Squire on the lawns of Steanbridge House on Peace Day 1919, and when a little older trudged at Christmas-time down the Squire's drive with a candle in a jam jar to sing carols in the porch.

The lane passes the gate of the manor, and a few yards further on runs by the village pond (877077), a sunken, reedy

The pond

sheet of semi-stagnant water surrounded by willows. Fred Bates the milkman discovered the naked body of poor crazed Miss Flynn floating among the lily-weeds of the pond early one morning, and gained himself a day's fame in every house in Slad. In winter the pond was the scene of skating and sliding expeditions for the whole neighbourhood, and Laurie and his friends would join in until they had played themselves beyond exhaustion far into the night.

Turn off the lane past the head of the pond and over a gate, and walk up the side of the field towards the trees at the top. The next field to the right (877075) is the scene of the most celebrated incident in *Cider with Rosie*, when sly and alluring Rosie Burdock met Laurie making hay after school one hot summer's afternoon. Her taunting eyes and ripe body fascinated and terrified Laurie, who fell powerless into her arms under a hay wagon. Concealed in the dusty darkness and drunk on stolen cider, Laurie spent a heavenly afternoon with Rosie — an afternoon that contained only one kiss, but a whole world of sensual delights. When he finally reached home late that night, soaked, stung and bruised after a riotous stumble homewards through the dusk, he sat on the chopping-block outside, bawling martial hymns until his brothers came and marched him off to bed.

Beside the pond the lane runs on, overlooked by the clump of trees on Down Hill and the handsome buildings of Down Farm ahead on its slope. At the pond's end you come to a cross-roads (878078) where an old track crosses the lane and winds uphill into the trees on the right. Ahead is Steanbridge Farm, a magnificent three-storey house with a face full of mullioned windows, now divided into several dwellings. Across the lane from Steanbridge Farm is a narrow strip of trees on a boggy streamside, the site of Sixpence Robinson's house (878079). Sixpence lived here with his beautiful sisters, Sis and Sloppy, and his brothers, Stosher and Sammy, the latter an agile crippled boy who played a fierce game of cricket in spite of his leg-irons. Laurie loved to spend long summer afternoons with Sixpence the Tanner, ducking Sixpence's pigeons in the water-butt and damming the stream with his gang of friends while Sis and Sloppy, a different proposition from Rosie Burdock and other village hussies, hid in the gooseberry patch from the scuffling boys.

From the crossroads you turn up the steep stony track to the left between beech and holly hedges. Slad on its slope is seen over to the left, three grand copper beeches adding a dark splash of colour to the view. The hedge banks are full of bluebells, violets and primroses in spring. Three-quarters of the way up the track, a gate on the right (877081) brings you out at the top of Twyning's Grove, whose edge you follow to the end of the trees. The footpath then skirts a deep combe where vines are planted on the south-facing slope. The view from the top of the combe is pure Cotswold — the rounded head of the valley, Trillgate Farm at your feet, the woods, hedges and houses each perfectly placed in its setting. It is a scene of harmonious beauty — but, like Francis Kilvert's Cwm near Clyro, the beauty hides a sinister beast. In the valley-bottom beyond Trillgate Farm lies the wood known to Laurie Lee as Deadcombe Bottom (882087), where the Bulls Cross hangman had once lived. This unfortunate had executed his own son by mistake one dark night on the nearby Bulls Cross gallows. On realizing the identity of his victim, the hangman had gone straight home to his house in Deadcombe Bottom and hanged himself from a hook behind the door. Laurie and his brothers discovered the ruins of the hangman's house one day and often returned to play there, swinging from the hook behind the door in ignorance of its grisly history.

To reach Bulls Cross bear left uphill above Trillgate Farm and follow the edge of the field for a few yards to a gap in the hedge, by which you gain the farm lane. Turn left and climb uphill past old woven sheep-hurdles to the crossroads on the crest of the ridge (877087).

Bulls Cross was an important meeting point of roads in years gone by, marked by an ancient stone cross whose weathered, three-tiered stump is in the verge to your right as you emerge from the farm lane. A rusty metal plate attached to the stump reads:

CHELT^m
II
STROUD
3

Bulls Cross

Stopping to get your breath back after the climb is a pleasure in this high and lonely spot six hundred feet up. The little grey stone town of Painswick straddles its ridge across the valley, the tall spire of the church making a natural focal point. Ninety-nine yews grow in the churchyard — local legend says that they have never been successfully counted. The vegetation up here is alien to the surrounding valleys, bracken and silver birch creating a heathland atmosphere. The Slad villagers reckoned Bulls Cross to be haunted by a runaway coach and horses, the sight of which could addle the brains of anyone unlucky enough to see it. Its ill-omened reputation probably owes a great deal to folk memories of the bodies of hanged felons, dispatched by the hangman of Deadcombe Bottom, which dangled here to admonish passers-by and feed the crows.

A couple of hundred yards along the road marked '*Sheepscombe 1$\frac{1}{2}$*' was the house that old Emmanuel Twinning shared with his skewbald horse (878090). Emmanuel wore home-made suits patched together out of hospital blankets, and was a figure of reverence to the young Laurie. John-Jack lived nearby, too, in incestuous domesticity with his sister, Nancy, and the five beautiful children they produced.

From Bulls Cross take the rough track on the left of the sloping lane marked '*Painswick 1*'. The gently climbing track leads off among the tall old beech trees of Frith Wood, named Brith Wood by Laurie Lee. Just beyond an ancient upright stone with a mason's mark in it (876086), take the left-hand path where the track divides, and bear left again in a few yards at another fork. Between the smooth trunks of the beeches you can look out over the fields and woods of the Slad valley.

Here in Brith Wood Laurie's gang lay in wait one Sunday for daft Lizzie Berkeley as she took her usual short cut home from chapel, chalking 'JESUS LOVES ME NOW' on the beech trunks as she went. None of the boys knew exactly what they were going to do to Lizzie, but vague lustings and thoughts of her dumpy body had been firing their imaginations since they had planned the ambush earlier in the week. When it came to the moment of action, however, Lizzie was more than a match for her assailants, and went into battle whirling her bag of crayons. She got home a couple of blows and trotted off unscathed, leaving the gang to melt away too embarrassed to look each other in the face.

The track continues downhill and along the bottom of the wood just above the main road. Soon it is joined by another path from higher up, and a few yards further on you bear left onto a narrow path (872081) with an old mossy stone wall on your left, which runs at the back of the cottage gardens of Slad. The path turns sharply downhill to leave the wood and join the main road by the Old Vicarage.

On the other side of the road is the War Memorial (873078), the site of a murder which was never solved. A village-boy-made-good returned from New Zealand one winter's evening, and made the mistake of bragging about his wealth to the public bar of the Woolpack. He went on to taunt the local young men for a crowd of stay-at-home peasants. When he left the pub in a blinding snowstorm the young men were waiting for him by the War Memorial. They beat and kicked him senseless, threw him over a wall and left him to freeze to death in the snow. The police tried to break through the barrier of silence that met their enquiries, but Slad turned a deaf ear to the outsiders and kept its dark secret to itself.

Just down the lane beside the War Memorial was the cottage

of Joseph and Hannah Brown, the self-sufficient, hardy old couple who lived a life untouched by the twentieth century, contented with each other and their daily round of chicken-feeding, wood-chopping, gardening and fruit-bottling. Then they both fell ill, were bundled off to the workhouse and found themselves separated for the first time in more than half a century. Authority had broken the shell of their lives, and within a week they were both dead. The cottage was a heap of stones within a year, crumbling to pieces as if in sympathy with the old couple. Now a bright new house occupies the site.

Turn right down the main road from the War Memorial and walk through the village past the Lees' house to the Church of the Holy Trinity (872073), high up above the road on the right in a grove of dark trees. The church was one of the foundation stones of the old village, with a lusty choir (of which Laurie was a member), an old-fashioned vicar of fire and brimstone and a packed congregation every Sunday. The interior is plain and cool, with four handsome stone arches on the left of the nave and an off-centre chancel. The Roll of Honour lists 20 men — an enormous toll from a small village — 3 of whom were killed in the last months of the war, and one of whom lingered on to die of his wounds a year later.

Along the road from the church is the village school (now a private house), a long, low building on the right which is protected from the road by a stone wall. Here Laurie received the rudimentary education of the day, and witnessed the humiliation of Crabby, the vinegary headmistress, a 'hunched-up little creature all spring-coils and slaps', who tormented the hulking slow-learners at the back of the class. One memorable day she went too far and was heaved up onto the top of the schoolroom cupboard by Spadge Hopkins. There she stayed, 'drumming her heels and weeping', while the little devils below stamped on the floor in derision. After that her power was broken, and when a new headmistress replaced her the schoolroom ceased to be a place of terror.

For one evening every year it was a place of delight for the villagers, when the Parochial Church Tea and Annual Entertainment took place. Introduced in broken mumblings by the Squire, the evening started with a mammoth tea at trestle-tables, then progressed through a programme of local talent that ranged from Laurie himself, scraping away in a fiddle-and-piano duet, through jokes and sketches to the performance of the Baroness von Hodenburg, all the way from Sheepscombe, who offered her own composition in celebration of 'ziss pleasant valleys':

> 'Elfin volk come over the hill!
> Come und dance, just vere you vill!
> Brink your pipes, und brink your flutes,
> Brink your sveetly soundink notes!
> Come avay-hay! Life is gay-hay!
> Life — Is — Gay!'

Most of the characters in *Cider with Rosie* thus neatly assembled under one roof, our walk ends. Across the road is the Woolpack Inn where the New Zealander sealed his fate with his loud mouth, and where you can buy copies of Laurie Lee's works with your pint, and chat to the present-day inhabitants of the village round which *Cider with Rosie* revolves.

Local Library
Stroud Library, Lansdown, Stroud, Glos GL5 1BL

Useful books
Cider with Rosie — Brodie's Notes — by Kenneth Hardacre.
Published by Pan Educational, 1976

A Walk in Kilvert Country

Kilvert's Diary, edited by William Plomer
First published in three volumes
by Jonathan Cape, 1938–1940
First published in a one-volume selection, 1944
Penguin paperback, 1977

(Clyro — Birds Nest Lane — Pen-y-cae — Bettws Chapel — Crowther's Pool — Newgate — Rhosgoch Common — Rhosgoch Mill — Plas-warren — The Hom — The Cwm — Sunny Bank — Fforest-cwm — Clyro. A fairly easy ten-mile round walk, mostly by lanes and footpaths. Farmers permit walkers to cross their land, provided that they are not accompanied by a dog.)

O.S.– 1:50,000 Sheet No. 148 'Presteign and Hay-on-Wye'
1:25,000 First Series, Sheets No. SO 24 'Hay-on-Wye' and SO 14 'Painscastle'

A mile and a half north-west of Hay-on-Wye, where the river Wye, that loveliest and most placid of rivers, marks the transition from Hereford's lush cattle pastures and cider apple orchards to the wild and sombre uplands of Powys, the little village of Clyro stands just inside the Welsh border with the hills at its back and the beautiful valley of the Wye at its feet. The whitewashed stone houses of old Clyro have been supplemented in recent years by an estate of modern houses, but it is still a sleepy and modest place which motorists on the new by-pass road from Hereford to Brecon might circumvent without a second glance. As they speed past the village, they might perhaps take in the grey tower of the church, the white bulk of the Baskerville Arms, and opposite it a tall plain stone house, handsome enough, but certainly nothing worth stopping for. Yet thousands of pilgrims every year leave the

Opposite: *Francis Kilvert in the photograph that hangs in Clyro Church*

by-pass to steer their cars through the narrow village street to the Baskerville Arms and Ashbrook House. Here, during seven golden years from 1865–72, lived Francis Kilvert, the curate of Clyro: a man who has been described as 'a St Francis in England and Wales', who once called himself 'an angel satyr', and who has left us in the pages of his diary probably the finest and most sensitive and lovingly observed account ever written of the daily life and characters of a small community.

But there is more to the diary than a meticulous, humorous and in many instances sublime series of descriptive passages. The man himself, romantic, warm, alive to the beauties of nature and young women, open to the joys and sufferings of his neighbours, grows more immediate and clearer in outline the further one reads, until by the end of the diary one seems to have known him in his raptures, depressions, love affairs and laughter as intimately as a living friend. He is not a paragon of virtue, or an uncritical enthuser, but a man full to bursting with a sense of life in all its moods, giving expression to exultation and misery, occasional bigotry and malice, far more frequent affection and understanding. The fact that so much of his personal writing still survives is itself a piece of extraordinary good fortune.

Robert Francis Kilvert was born on 3rd December 1840, at Hardenhuish (pronounced Harnish), a small village near Chippenham, Wiltshire, where his father, Robert Kilvert, was rector. Robert Kilvert had established a school in Hardenhuish Rectory which the young Francis attended; not a particularly happy or liberated school, according to one of the old boys, Augustus Hare:

'Mr Kilvert . . . was deeply religious, but was very hot-tempered, and slashed our hands with a ruler and our bodies with a cane most unmercifully for exceedingly slight offences. So intense, so abject was our terror of him that we used to look forward as to an oasis the one afternoon he went on his parish duties.'

Francis left his father's school for another at Claverton Lodge, near Bath, run by his uncle Francis, a scholar, writer and poet. He was at Wadham College, Oxford, from 1859–62, graduated with a poor 4th Class BA and went to help his father with his duties at Langley Burrell, a parish a few miles from Hardenhuish to which living the Reverend Robert had been presented in 1855. In 1864 Francis was ordained, and continued to act as curate to his father until 1865, when he went to Clyro as curate to the Reverend Richard Lister Venables, an intelligent and hard-working parish priest. Kilvert lodged at Ashbrook House with Mrs Chaloner, and remained there with her throughout his seven-year curacy at Clyro. There he began in 1870 the diary that was to become his great pleasure and solace, particularly in the years after 1872 when, exiled from his beloved Clyro, he struggled to capture the sheer joy in life and sense of purpose that shines out of every page of the Clyro entries.

The Clyro to which the 24-year-old Kilvert came was in many ways a backward and narrow-minded place of pre-Industrial Revolution values. In England as a whole the old agricultural base of society was collapsing, and the full effects of the Industrial Revolution and of improved means of transport were being felt. Although Kilvert appreciated and used to the full the new railway that had been opened through Hay the previous year, Clyro itself was a backwater where the farm workers and cottagers still lived lives strongly influenced by superstition, violence, poverty, incurable sickness and early death, rather like the villagers of Haworth in the Brontës' days, though they were more welcoming and affectionate to their visitors! Illegitimate pregnancy was still a frightful stigma which drove many a young girl to infanticide or suicide; folk remedies for illnesses were the rule rather than the exception; insane relatives were incarcerated in upstairs rooms and left to rant and roar by themselves. Although Kilvert's eyes and heart were open to the tribulations of the poorest folk in the way that Parson Woodforde's never were, Woodforde's local persons of consequence such as the Howeses, Jeanses, Townshends and Mr Du Quesne found their parallel a century later with Kilvert's Bevans, Morrells, Thomases and Crichtons, families with whom a poor curate was only too pleased to socialize; while Squire Walter Baskerville of Clyro Court seems to have been just as kindly and well-intentioned a landlord as Squire Custance of Weston House.

Kilvert was a dedicated and conscientious visitor of his poor parishioners — 'villaging' as he called it — and his diary bears witness to the pleasure both parties took in these visits. A great favourite was the 'old Peninsular veteran' John Morgan, who lived at the Bronith (now spelt Bronydd), a hamlet a mile or so north-east of Clyro.

> *Tuesday, 26th April 1870*: 'John Morgan was tottering about his garden with crutches, gathering stones off the beds and hoeing the earth between the potato rows. I took the hoe from the old soldier and hoed three rows for him, finishing the patch. Then we went indoors and sat down by the fire.'

In between parish visits and taking services in the Church of St Michael and All Angels and the little chapel-of-ease of Bettws three miles away up the hill, Kilvert played croquet, tennis and archery, attended balls, card parties and Penny Readings, and went out walking and driving with his well-to-do neighbours. He was also a great solitary walker and gatherer of wild flowers, delighting in the wildness and loneliness of the hill country behind Clyro. Wordsworth's romantic ideal of natural beauty affected Kilvert deeply from his first contact with the poet of Lakeland, and stirred him to those heights of descriptive genius that give the diary's writing its special quality.

> *Friday, 11th February 1870*: 'Coming back [from Hay] the hills were lovely. The morning spread upon the mountains, beautiful Clyro rising from the valley and stretching away northward dotted with white houses and shining with gleams of greens on hills and dingle sides, a tender blue haze over the village and woods in the valley and Clyro Court a dim grey.'

> *Friday, 13th October 1871*: 'Round the great dark heather-clothed shoulder of the mountain swept the green ride descending steeply to the Fuallt farm and fold and the valley opened still more wide and fair. The beautiful Glasnant came leaping and rushing down its lovely dingle, a flood of molten silver and crystal fringed by groups of silver birches and alders, and here and there a solitary tree rising from the bright green sward along the banks of the brook and drooping over the stream which seemed to come out of a fairy land of blue valley depths and distances and tufted woods of green and gold and crimson and russet brown.'

Wednesday, 7th February 1872: 'I walked to Hay. The afternoon was brilliant in its loveliness. The sun was under a cloud from behind which streamed seven broad rays onto the variegated mountain and valley, river and meadow, striking out brilliant gems of sunlit emerald green on the hill sides.'

Kilvert seems to have been a stirring preacher, judging by the few fragments of commentary on his sermons that he makes; in the theories of his trade, a moderate, suspicious of extreme high and low church stances; as a man, beloved and trusted by the humbler members of his flock, accepted readily enough by his social superiors.

The darker side of his nature, freely admitted and often castigated by himself, has been the subject of much speculation since his diary was first published. There is no doubt that Kilvert loved and sought the company of little girls to an unusual extent. He wrote in ecstasies of joy about chance meetings or sightings, savouring in retrospect kisses and cuddles with little girls at the school and farmstead.

Wednesday, 23rd August 1871: 'I had not been long in the house when Hannah's beautiful seven-year-old child Carrie gradually stole up to me and nestled close in my arms. Then she laid her warm temples and soft round cheek lovingly to mine and stole first one arm then the other round my neck. Her arms tightened round my neck and she pressed her face closer and closer to mine, kissing me again and again. . . An hour flew like a few seconds. I was in heaven. . . I was lost to everything but love and the embrace and the sweet kisses and caresses of the child. It seemed as if we could not part we loved each other so. . . When I went away she brought me the best flower she could find in the garden. I am exhausted with emotion.'

These words, written that night by Kilvert in his room at Ashbrook House, are nearer the feverish recollections of a passionate lover than the diary entry of a visiting curate. However, it must be remembered that Kilvert, a man of extremely sensuous nature, was perforce a bachelor by reason of the poverty in which a Victorian curate lived, and had all Wordsworth's romanticism and the sexual frustration of his situation working overtime on his always highly charged emotions. There was no other outlet for them; certainly the young ladies in his life would never have permitted the unin-hibited public embraces that his adored children allowed him.

On Friday, 8th September, 1871, Kilvert made the following entry in his diary: 'Today I fell in love with Fanny Thomas.'

Fanny, or Daisy as Kilvert usually refers to her, lived at Llanthomas, a few miles out of Hay-on-Wye. She grew to feel warmly towards the romantic young curate, but her father, the Reverend William Jones Thomas, Vicar of Llanigon, knew very well what were the likely prospects of such a suitor. After a courtship of delicious moments and long agonized speculations on the part of Kilvert, he was gently but firmly forbidden to think of an engagement by Mr Thomas, and the relationship flickered out into what was either an honourable self-denial or a rather hurtful neglect by Francis of his lover — who eventually died in 1928, still unmarried.

This sadly broken affair was probably the most important factor in influencing Kilvert to leave Clyro in 1872 and return to Langley Burrell for another spell as curate to his ailing, nearly deaf father. There followed four years of patient, dedicated ministry, recorded in the diary with flashes of the old delight but lacking the magic of his Clyro years. Another love affair, with Ettie Meredith Brown, who possessed a 'dark Spanish brunette complexion with its rich glow of health which gave her cheeks the dusky bloom and flush of a ripe pomegranate', also ended in Kilvert being forbidden to communicate with her again, this time by the mother.

In 1876 Kilvert accepted the living of the neglected, run-down and remote parish of St Harmon, about four miles north of Rhayader, and for a year did his best to restore a disenchanted flock's faith in its shepherd. Then in 1877 he became Vicar of Bredwardine, a few miles east of Clyro, and returned to the countryside and people that lay nearest his heart. Two years of fulfilment lay ahead, as Kilvert's parishioners found their vicar as true and steadfast a friend as had the folk of Clyro their young curate.

On 20th August 1879, those years of passionate romanticism flowered into reality when Kilvert married Elizabeth Anne Rowland, whom he had probably met three years earlier on a trip to Paris. She was not as pretty or lively as Daisy or Ettie, but a pleasant and kind-hearted woman, and Kilvert's

satisfaction and happiness were evident in the replies he made
to the speeches and gifts that greeted him and his bride when
they returned to Bredwardine after their honeymoon journey
to Edinburgh. The happy pair were drawn, in a cart harnessed
to local men, between floral arches to the Vicarage, where a
deputation of farmers presented him with half a dozen silver
dessert spoons and forks. Kilvert was especially, and typically,
touched by the next gift of a pair of silver gravy spoons from the
cottagers of Bredwardine, saying: 'Much as I am taken by
surprise by the last beautiful gift from my friends who occupy
good positions in life, this touches me more deeply still,
because I know that it is given from slender incomes and
pockets not very deep. This beautiful gift has, I believe, been
prompted by a love which I feel I very little deserve.' (No, No.)
'But if God spares me I will try to deserve your affection and
show you how deeply grateful I am for these kind efforts
today.' (Applause)

Unfortunately God did not spare him. Kilvert had been in
increasingly poor health since his return to the Wye Valley,
changing in a few years from the vigorous young curate who
thought nothing of walking twenty miles or more in all
weathers over the hills, to a feeble, prematurely aged man who
suffered almost continuously from coughs, colds and sore
throats. Five short weeks after his marriage he contracted
peritonitis, and died on Tuesday, 23rd September 1879, aged
thirty-eight. His grave in Bredwardine churchyard faces down
the valley towards the long rise of Bredwardine Knapp,
engraved simply; '*He being dead yet speaketh*'.

Mrs Kilvert did not die until 1911. As her husband's grave
was by that time closely flanked by those of two of his
benefactors, she was buried in a far corner of the churchyard —
modest and obscure in death as in life. However, she did make
her mark in the Kilvert story in one dramatic and regrettable
way; for she destroyed two large chunks of the diary (9th
September 1875—1st March 1876, and 27th June 1876—31st
December 1877), apparently because they contained intimate
references to Kilvert's courtship of her and of Ettie Meredith
Brown. On her death, she bequeathed the remaining 22
notebooks to Francis's sister, Dora, with instructions to burn
them. However, Dora appreciated their value and did not

carry out her sister-in-law's wishes.

Some time later they came into the possession of Mrs Kilvert's nephew, Perceval Smith. He, too, realised the significance of the diaries and sent the notebooks to Jonathan Cape, the publishers. One of their readers, William Plomer, made a typescript of the whole surviving diary before returning the notebooks to Perceval Smith, and prepared a series of extracts which were published in three volumes (1938, 1939 and 1940). They travelled round the world with servicemen during the war, and achieved enormous popularity as the reading public became acquainted with Clyro, Langley Burrell and Bredwardine, and characters such as Gipsy Lizzie and the Solitary of Llanbedr — and above all, Kilvert himself.

At some stage during the war, William Plomer decided to destroy his typescript of the diary, confident that the 22 original notebooks were in good hands. This was a tragic error, as things turned out; for the notebooks passed from Perceval Smith to his sister, Essex Smith, who was more concerned with the dubious morality of some of the entries than with their literary, historical or human merit. She had enjoyed a brief vogue as a novelist between the wars; and either pique at her forebear's much greater fame, or a genuine desire to see the 'satyr' suppressed, caused her to destroy all but three of the notebooks. One of these has since proved untraceable, but the other two still survive.

William Plomer, himself, while mourning the loss of both source material and his own copy, felt that he had done Kilvert and Kilvert-lovers a favour by publishing only the very best of the diary. In his lecture at the inaugural meeting of the Kilvert Society on 17th July 1948, he made this clear: 'My business was to sort out the grain from the chaff. . . I left out what seemed to me commonplace and trivial, so you only know Kilvert at his most vivid.'

Although the diary as it stands today represents Kilvert only as seen through the filter of William Plomer's selections, such is the quality of the diarist's work (and that of his editor as well) that we can discover the places and people of 1870 on a walk in Kilvert country in the company of the curate of Clyro.

*　　*　　*

Ashbrook House

The north wall of Ashbrook House (214438) bears a simple slate plaque recording Kilvert's residence there. From his bedroom he could hear the merriment across the road at the Swan Inn (now the Baskerville Arms) when Clyro Feast Ball was held there on 18th October 1870.

> 'As I write I hear the scraping and squealing of the fiddle and the ceaseless heavy tramp of the dancers as they stamp the floor in a country dance.'

The squealing fiddles have been replaced by electric guitars at the Baskerville Arms, where bored local bands croon hits of twenty years ago to the backs of diners' heads; but the building is largely the one that Kilvert knew, where after Hay Fair the farmers who had sold nothing would gather to drown their sorrows in an atmosphere deplored by the diarist:

'There will be an explosion in a minute. It only wants one word, a spark. Here it is. Someone had said something. A sudden blaze of passion, a retort, a word and a blow, a rush, a scuffle, a Babel of voices, a tumult, the furious voices of the combatants rising high and furious above the din.'

He records men 'lying by the roadside all night, drunk, cursing, muttering, maundering and vomiting.'

From these unsavoury scenes we pass eastwards beneath the steep green slope behind the inn, known to Kilvert as the Bron, up which he walked on 16th March 1870, having eaten so much hare that he could hardly walk and saw stars. Three months later a tar barrel was set ablaze on the Bron to celebrate the birth of Mrs Venables' daughter.

Turn uphill to the left at the road junction (215439), passing New House on your right where Mr Thomas, the 'cutter' or itinerant lamb castrator, lived — hence Cutter's Pitch, the name of the sharply rising lane. Broomfield, the house opposite, stands on the site of 'The Brooms', where Kilvert went on 15th April 1871 to read to the owner, Sackville Thomas. The little girl Polly stripped herself for the tub in front of him 'with great celerity and satisfaction', affording him 'a most interesting view from the rear'.

Cutter's Pitch climbs between high banks topped with hedges in which bracken, broom and tall foxgloves soon appear. The view to the right opens out above the hedges across to Lower House Farm, and above it to Court Evan Gwynne, where they kept up the old tradition of hanging sprigs of birch and wittan over the 'great old fashioned house door'. Two mighty oak trees guard the entrance to the drive of Court Evan Gwynne (215447), overshadowing a fine open-sided barn with wooden struts on a stone base, roofed with slates. The lane dips down into tree-lined valleys and climbs out again, a typical feature of the Welsh border country, where the focus of the landscape is constantly changing from far-flung views to small-scale details near at hand. Hereabouts orchids grow in colonies in the banks of the lane, which passes whitewashed Cwm Bythog and comes to the entrance of Birds Nest Lane on the left, marked '*Upper Wernypentre*' (217451).

Grass grows through the tarmac of Birds Nest Lane, up

which we follow the footsteps of the curate to Mrs Bowen's house and to the Williamses at Little Wern-y-pentre. Kilvert's description still holds good: 'It is a pretty lane, this Birds Nest Lane, very shady and quiet, narrow and overbowered here and there with arching wyches and hazels.'

There was another reason for his raptures over Birds Nest Lane, for this was the path to the school in Clyro of the most beloved of all his beloved little girls, Gipsy Lizzie, 'my darling Gipsy' with her 'dark large beautiful eyes and a dazzling smile showing her little white teeth, as she tossed her dark curls back'. In his entry for 9th July 1870 he speculated on how many times her tiny feet had trodden 'this stony narrow green-arched lane', and went on: 'If you only knew that this lane and this dingle and these fields are sweet to me and holy ground for your sweet sake.'

In July the flowers that Gipsy Lizzie plucked on her way to school still grow in Birds Nest Lane — speedwell, campion, foxgloves, ragged robin, vetch, buttercups, forget-me-nots and more orchids. We tread Kilvert's 'holy ground' as far as Little Wern-y-pentre, a house set back on the right where the lane divides (213455). One fork carries straight on to Upper Wern-y-pentre, and the other turns sharp right. On Lady Day (25th March) 1871, Kilvert visited the old Williamses at Little Wern-y-pentre and heard of the murder of Price of Cwmrafan by his would-be son-in-law, and of the doing to death of an illegitimate baby at the Bronith. It was snowing so hard that old Mrs Williams insisted on giving the curate her shawl to protect his shoulders on the way home.

You take the right-hand fork in the lane and walk up with a splendid view on the right of the Black Mountains. Turn left on reaching the road and continue to climb to Pen-y-cae, home of Gipsy Lizzie (211467), which now accommodates campers. Up here curlews and crying lambs characterize the moorland scenery, in which the crooked slate-roofed shed and sturdy farmhouse of Pen-y-cae overlook the Wye Valley, with abandoned iron farm machinery from the horse age littering the farmyard. Gipsy Lizzie's legs, however attractive, must have been pretty solid to carry her the six miles down the hill and back every day. Just before the house of Ty-nesa, take the lane to the right marked 'Rhydspence' (212469), passing an ancient, wind-tattered fir and the gate on the left to Pant-y-cae. Here Kilvert found no one at home on 3rd May 1870, so 'stuck a cowslip in the latch hole by way of leaving a card'. Before coming to Pant-y-cae he had visited the site of Whitehall, a ruined old farm reached by the next lane on the right. Today the building (215467) is a shell of tumble-down walls and tinder-dry wooden beams, and Kilvert found it in not much better repair: 'Poor Whitehall, sad, silent and lonely, with its great black yew in the hedge of the tangled waste grass-grown garden, and its cold chimney still ivy-clustered.'

Many a lonely young drover put up at the Black Ox, a nearby inn, and local girls seem to have enjoyed courting them. Kilvert reminisced over the quarterly dances held at Whitehall, with their 'laughing, flirting, joking and kissing behind the door or in the dark garden amongst the young folks', which had given way to 'the wind sighing through the broken roof and crazy doors. . . a deathlike stillness about the place'.

Rejoining the lane, you walk on past Pen-yr-heol ('top of the road') where scrap cars line the verges, with a tremendous view ahead of the hills of Herefordshire. The lane passes the farm of Llwyn-gwilliam away to the left, crosses the signposted route of Offa's Dyke, or 'Llwybr Clawdd Offa', and comes to Bettws Chapel, dark, plain, and half-hidden among gloomy trees to the right (228473). A stony track opposite a bungalow named Aylton Lea, where the key to the chapel can be obtained, leads to the obscure path by the side of a cornfield that brings you to the only gate in the barbed-wire fence around the chapel. Two very stiff doors admit you to the dark, cool interior, with a floor in patterned tiles and a roof supported by massive cross-beams. There is no mention anywhere of Francis Kilvert, who regularly walked the three miles or more from Clyro, all uphill, to take services at this chapel-of-ease. He perfectly described the surroundings in his diary entry for 9th July 1871:

'In the chapel field the tall brown and purple grasses were all in billows like the sea, as the wind coursed over the hill driving one billow after another, sheen and dusk, up against the chapel wall. And the chapel in the grass looked like a house founded upon a rock in the midst of a billowy sea.'

110

The weather could be savagely cold, as on 13th February 1870, when he 'went to Bettws in the afternoon wrapped in two waistcoats, two coats, a muffler and a mackintosh, and was not at all too warm. When I got to the chapel my beard moustaches and whiskers were so stiff with ice that I could hardly open my mouth and my beard was frozen on to my mackintosh.'

By contrast, on Easter Day the same year, 'it was burning hot and as I climbed the hill the perspiration rolled off my forehead from under my hat and fell in drops on the dusty road.'

When he took his last service at Bettws on 25th August 1872, he broke down and cried while preaching on the text 'I thank my God upon every remembrance of you' (Philippians 1, 3).

On regaining the road, turn right and walk round the bend of the road. Take the next footpath on the left over the fields to join the road again opposite the farm of Cae-Higgin (228478). Turn left here and carry on over the brook and up, bearing left at the next road junction to pass the house of Cwm-yr-eithin. Continue over the crossroads above Crowther's Pool with its scattered houses. Beyond Crowther's Pool you pass on your left the old lane (213483) leading to Hearts Ease, where lived Henry Warnell the gypsy, who got six weeks' hard labour in 1870 for kicking Price of the Swan 'in the bad place' and tearing a stout pair of corduroy trousers.

To the north there are fine upland views of Newchurch Hill and Bryngwyn Hill above the valley along whose floor lies 'the black and gloomy peat bog, the Rhos Goch, with the dark cold gleam of the stagnant water among its mawn pits, the graves of the children'. To reach a viewpoint over this mournful spot, turn right on to the Newchurch to Clyro road at Newgate, and walk up to the B4594 Newchurch to Rhosgoch road. Turn left here and carry on towards the hamlet of Rhosgoch, looking down on the bog, which supports a thick forest of bushes on its treacherous, scummy surface. Local legend says that a great town lies below the bog, swallowed up in a cataclysm long ago. Kilvert recorded another tale of a great battle at the Rhos Goch ('Red Common'), provoked by the Giant of Painscastle. This monster abducted a Miss Phillips whom he found 'disporting herself with her lover Arthur'. Arthur had the bad luck to kill his girlfriend by mistake as she was escaping from

Painscastle dressed as a man. 'Arthur then furious stormed the castle with a battle-axe: took it and killed the giant.' Honour being even, the opposing forces met the next day at the Rhos Goch and the decider was fought out at Rhyd Llyden nearby, with Arthur's army emerging victorious. Skeletons from a great battle are still being unearthed there today.

It is a gloomy and ominous place where local children were frequently drowned in Kilvert's day. On the far slope stands the lonely farmhouse of Llanshiver (200477) — Llys Ivor, or 'Ivor's Court' — a place of importance in bygone days when at least three roads converged on the moated farmstead. There, on 16th March 1870, Kilvert was entertained in the damp, dark kitchen to tea and cake by Mrs Morgan, after which her husband conducted him over the remains of the moat where the body of a Scottish pedlar was hidden after he had been murdered in the house for the contents of his pack.

You pass the chapel at Rhosgoch to reach Rhos Goch Mill (185475) a few hundred yards further along on the left and set back below the level of the road — 'a cosy old picturesque ivy-grown millhouse with its tall chimney completely covered with ivy'. Here, on 26th March 1870, Kilvert was greeted by the young miller, Mr Powell, 'with the most perfect politeness and well bred courtesy'. Mr Powell was only about sixteen years old at the time, and lived on until the 1950s; he is still well remembered in the area. Kilvert took delight in the story of 'the old man who slept in the mill trough at the Rhos Goch Mill and used to hear the fairies come in at night and dance to sweet fiddles on the mill floor.'

Now retrace your steps to Rhosgoch Chapel, opposite which turn right and continue along the Clyro road, which climbs out of the valley past the farmstead of Pentre (191472), often visited by Kilvert. Tussocks of sedge appear in the fields each side of the road, which after a long haul finally tops out; here you are rewarded with the best long-distance view of the walk, with the far blue hills of Herefordshire to the left, the Brecon Beacons away to the right, and ahead the frowning ramparts of the Black Mountains with little Hay-on-Wye dwarfed at their feet. You can feast your eyes on this splendid panorama as you descend the long road to Plas-warren farm, below which is a crossroads (202456) just above a very isolated telephone box.

Rhos Goch Mill

Turn right here and walk along the winding lane till you come to a brown brick bungalow on your right (192454). Turn left opposite this, down a steep lane in whose brackeny hedge lies the rusting hulk of a vintage green-painted Morris Commercial lorry, now used as a petrol bowser by the vehicle hire and repair business at the Hom, the farm at the end of the lane (191449). Mr Herdman, the owner, will readily give permission (but please do ask first at the house) for walkers to go through the gate at the front of the house, bear left and downwards across the field and join his track which leads on down past a large ash tree at the bottom of the field.

The old sunken lane which Kilvert often used to visit the Hom is now impassable and overgrown below the newly cut track. The gentle curate grew to love the Cwm, this utterly quiet, tree-lined valley where nowadays the only sounds to be heard are bird-song and the trickle of the Clyro Brook in the valley-bottom — when they are not revving engines at the Hom! But Kilvert, for all his rhapsodizing, knew a different and darker side to the Cwm — for the four dwellings there produced between them three suicides and two mad women.

On the other side of the track from the great ash tree is a heap of stones, all that remains of Burnt House (192448), where Grandmother Phillips hanged herself behind the door on hearing the news of her granddaughter's suicide. Anne Phillips, in service at Clyro Court, threw herself into the Wye after being tormented by the other servants over the imprisonment of her father. A few hundred yards further down the valley is New Barn (195445), high up on the bank to the left, where lived Mary Meredith, sister of John Meredith of the Hom and mother of an illegitimate baby boy by Bill Price of nearby Sunny Bank. Brother John would not allow her to draw the money from the bank with which she hoped to entice Bill Price to marry her. Mary 'seeing no hope of marriage became melancholy mad'. She, too, ended her misery in the cold waters of the Wye.

Across the valley from New Barn is the beautifully situated farm of Cwm-gwanon (191442) with its walled garden. Upstairs in 'a fetid room darkened' was locked mad old Mrs Watkins, whose roars could be heard in the dingle half a mile away, and who 'amuses herself by dancing naked round the room and threatens to wring her daughter-in-law's neck.' When Kilvert paid a visit on 31st August 1871, he found 'a mad skeleton with such a wild scared animal's face as I never saw before. Her dark hair was tossed weird and unkempt, and she stared at me like a wild beast.' He said the Lord's Prayer with her, and she begged him to come again. Then Kilvert went on up the valley to the Hom, where John Meredith's sister 'has been taken in a very queer way and seems to have gone out of her mind.'

You leave this lovely but haunted valley by the gate below New Barn, following the lane and turning right at the Clyro Road, which falls steeply towards the village and bends left below Fforest-cwm (198438). Kilvert knew this house as White Ash and often visited two old women there, Sarah Probert and her friend Hannah Jones, who smoked a short black pipe and had a dark-haired daughter whose liberally displayed charms the curate admired greatly. Sarah and Hannah spent a good deal of time 'groaning and rolling in bed'. When Kilvert told

Sarah to cheer up she called him a 'rum 'un' and a 'Job's comfort'. However, he discovered the cure for their ailments on 13th April 1872, when he 'gave them some money and their cries and groans suddenly ceased.'

After a long mile by road the roofs and chimneys of Clyro come into view and you drop down a street to the Church of St Michael and All Angels in the centre of the village. The church was largely rebuilt in 1852, so Kilvert knew it much as it is today. Characteristically, he most enjoyed preaching to the ordinary Clyro folk, as on Palm Sunday, 1872.

'In the afternoon I had the happiness to have all the poor people to myself. None of the grand people were at Church by reason of the snow. So of course I could speak much better and more freely.'

St Michael and All Angels, Clyro

At Easter two years before, the graves had been decked with flowers by the parishioners and looked 'as if the people had laid down just to sleep for the night out of doors, ready dressed to rise early on Easter morning.'

The interior contains plain, low box-pews on a diamond-tiled floor. There are Venables and Baskerville memorials, as well as a simple one to the diarist, inscribed '*Thou good and faithful servant*'.

You can complete your walk in his company by studying the only known photograph of the curate of Clyro, which hangs in the church. It is also reproduced on the cover of Frederick Grice's invaluable book, *Francis Kilvert and his World* (published by Caliban Books), by far the most comprehensive guide to Kilvert, his life, writing, loves, neighbours and contemporary society. The photograph shows a heavily bearded, pensive young man with a broad, dark brow, firm mouth and deep-set eyes, seated with one arm resting on an octagonal table, his finger lightly marking the place in the book on his knee — perhaps the current notebook of his diary (its future world-wide fame undreamed of by its creator), which has just received yet another confidence on the subject of his bewitching Gipsy Lizzie:

'But you can never know, and if you should ever guess or read the secret, it will be but a dim misty suspicion of the truth. Ah Gipsy.'

The Kilvert Society
c/o The Hon. Secretary, 27 Baker's Oak, Lincoln Hill, Ross-on-Wye, Herefordshire
Formed in 1948 to foster an interest in the Reverend Francis Kilvert, his work, his diary and the countryside he loved. Three newsletters annually. Activities include: AGM and social evening, summer and autumn commemoration services at churches with Kilvertian associations, three walks a year. The Society holds a large collection of photographs, and publishes booklets and cards.

Local Library
The Public Library, Hay-on-Wye
Hereford Public Library holds a substantial Kilvert archive.

Useful books
Francis Kilvert and his World by Frederick Grice. Published by
Caliban Books, 1982
Twenty-Four Walks in the Kilvert Country by M.M. Morgan.
Published by the Kilvert Society

To *Wuthering Heights* with Emily Brontë

Wuthering Heights by Emily Brontë
First published 1847
Penguin paperback, 1970

(The Brontë Parsonage Museum — the Brontë Falls — Top Withens [Wuthering Heights] — Ponden Hall [Thrushcross Grange] — Stanbury — Brontë Parsonage Museum. About seven miles by moorland paths, a short stretch of the Pennine Way and minor roads. In fine weather, a walk for anyone in walking clothes and footwear; during or after rain the paths can be very boggy; in mist, not a walk for the inexperienced)

O.S.– 1:50,000 Sheets Nos. 104 'Leeds & Bradford' and 103 'Blackburn & Burnley'
1:25,000 Outdoor Leisure Map 'South Pennines'

The industrial West Riding of Yorkshire, with the great untidy sprawl of Bradford at its heart, represents to most outsiders the ugliest face of the Industrial Revolution. Grim acres of tightly packed terraces, heavy engineering works and textile mills, sprawling towns running one into the next, inhabitants of few words and fewer airs and graces — these are the widely held impressions of an area where the Industrial Revolution brought hundreds of thousands of poorly paid workers to the new, hastily built and shabbily furnished, terraced back-to-backs that still climb up and down the hillsides. Nowadays, with mills and engineering works closing and school-leavers facing indefinite unemployment, the local people have to dig deep into those traditional reserves of Yorkshire men and women — kindness, steadfastness and

Opposite: *Emily Brontë by P.B. Brontë, courtesy*
NATIONAL PORTRAIT GALLERY

blunt humour — and cling ever more jealously to the other three virtues of the area — good pudding, good beer and good cricket.

As you go north-west from Bradford, however, the overlying carpet of Industrial Revolution buildings begins to wear thin and the bare boards of the countryside to show through. At Keighley the industrial sprawl is on its last legs and the far prospect is of high country, green fields separated by the spindly ever-curving lines of drystone walls that run up to a skyline of bleak and lonely moorland. At Keighley railway station British Rail hands over the reins to the shiny, carefully maintained steam locomotives and old-fashioned rolling stock of the Keighley and Worth Valley Railway. Travelling up the valley of the river Worth, which runs south-west away from Keighley, past the flower-beds and neat buildings of the railway stations, each mile takes you further into rural Yorkshire, the terraces and mills spaced further and further apart by farmland. The fourth station down the line is Haworth (pronounced 'Howarth') where nearly a million visitors a year come to climb the steep and narrow main street with its craft shops and galleries. At first sight of the valley-bottom, Haworth seems to have experienced the same development as the other towns and villages in the district — terraced houses, mills and factories jostle for position above the river. But from

Main Street, Haworth

the bottom of Main Street the scene changes. The dark canyon of weathered stone houses which mounts up the hillside has remained virtually unchanged for more than two centuries. The river, its running water a potent source of energy, attracted the new textile cathedrals of the Industrial Revolution — the mills — and left the higher portions of the village untouched by the great upheaval. The cottage weavers moved downhill or further afield to Keighley, Bradford, Halifax and Huddersfield; their houses in the upper main street can be identified by the long rows of narrow windows in the third storey that let in light to the weaving rooms. At the top of the street is the small but well-laid-out Tourist Information Centre, where among booklets and maps you can pick up a free leaflet, entitled with true Yorkshire abruptness: 'How to Stop Yourself Dying on the Moors'. It is a blunt reminder of the dangers of the inhospitable high countryside that surrounds the village.

The Georgian sandstone Parsonage stands on a stretch of level ground at the summit of the village, facing the church over a large graveyard of tall, green-lichened gravestones. In front are the houses of Haworth, descending the hill in dark layers of roofs and chimneys; behind the Parsonage, bare moorland rolls upwards to the skyline. To the cure of souls in this insular, isolated village in 1820 came Patrick Brontë, a self-educated Irishman, born Patrick Brunty in a two-roomed cabin in County Down, who had tenaciously grappled his way upwards via St John's College, Cambridge, and a BA Degree to ordination and a series of curacies in Essex, Shropshire and West Yorkshire. He brought with him his ailing wife, Maria, and six young children: Maria, Elizabeth, Charlotte, Branwell, Emily and Anne. Within eighteen months Mrs Brontë was dead, and from then on Mr Brontë led a regular and austere life at the Parsonage, working and dining apart from the rest of his family. Although he ate other meals with his children, and conscientiously oversaw their upbringing and education, much of the day-to-day care of his five daughters and only son was left to his sister-in-law, Miss Elizabeth Branwell, and a devoted servant, elderly Tabitha Aykroyd.

Their narrow, and by modern standards neglected, but far from unhappy childhoods were brought to a close when the four oldest children — Maria, Elizabeth, Charlotte and Emily — were sent to the Clergy Daughters' School at Cowan Bridge in 1824. By June 1825 Maria and Elizabeth had followed their mother to the grave, victims of the harsh regime, bad food and freezing cold of the school. Charlotte and Emily were brought home to Haworth, and for the next ten years the four surviving Brontë children stayed together in the Parsonage, apart from an eighteen-month period for Charlotte at Roe Head School. In 1835 the close-knit family group broke up and the brother and three sisters embarked on their adult lives. Branwell, Mr Brontë's only son, studied with a Leeds artist, William Robinson. In 1835 he went to London to apply for entry to the Royal Academy Schools, but his nerve failed and after an evening's drinking he returned home. A venture in painting portraits in a studio in Bradford likewise came to nothing, and he had spells as a railway clerk at the nearby Sowerby Bridge and Luddenden Foot stations before being dismissed in 1842 for book-keeping irregularities and time-wasting. By now he had begun to drink heavily. In 1843 he went as tutor to the Robinson household at Thorp Green in the Plain of York, where Anne had been governess for the past two years. A cloud of scandal burst in 1845, linking Branwell with Mrs Robinson, and he came home in disgrace to spend the last three years of his life drinking in the Black Bull Hotel in Haworth, taking opium and gradually succumbing to the family weakness, tuberculosis, or consumption as it was then called. On 24th September 1848 he died aged thirty-one, a raddled wreck of brilliant promise unfulfilled.

Charlotte, the oldest sister, went in 1835 to Roe Head School as a teacher. In 1838 the school moved to a damp location at Dewsbury Moor, and Charlotte's unhappiness with her situation increased until she made up her mind to leave. The next year she had two brief and miserable months as governess with Mrs Sidgwick at Gateshead Hall, Stonegappe, near Skipton, and in 1841 a further and rather happier period with the White family at Rawdon, near Bradford. In February 1842, having decided to open a school at the Parsonage with her sisters, she went with Emily to improve her languages at the Maison d'Education pour les Jeunes Demoiselles in Brussels. In October of that year Aunt Branwell died, and the sisters returned home; but Charlotte went back to Brussels in 1843 for a tortured year of teaching unmanageable girls (she was only 4ft 9ins tall) and silent, agonizing love for the handsome proprietor of the school, Monsieur Heger. In January 1844 she nerved herself to make the break from the unresolvable situation (Monsieur Heger was married with three children), and came home to Haworth to nurse her father through a cataract operation in 1846 and continuing ill-health. For the next eight years she lived an increasingly lonely life at the Parsonage, particularly after the trauma of losing her brother and two sisters to the killer consumption within the space of eight months between September 1848 and May 1849. In 1854, having previously rejected two proposals, she married the Reverend Arthur Bell Nicholls, whom she had known as curate of Haworth for the past ten years, much against the wishes of her father. On 31st March 1855, having caught cold walking in a rainstorm, she died aged thirty-eight, newly pregnant.

Emily's attempts to leave home, born of financial necessity, were brief and unhappy. In 1835 she spent three desperate months of home-sickness at Roe Head School, in 1837–8 a further period (it is uncertain exactly how long) as a governess at Law Hill near Halifax. Being away from home tormented her, as did having her liberty curtailed in any way. After the stay with Charlotte in Brussels at Monsieur Heger's Academy, she returned thankfully to Haworth and her domestic duties, until the claws of consumption finally dragged her down to death on 19th December 1848, less than three months after her brother.

Anne, the youngest sister, was the most successful at getting on in the outside world, though mild and shy in manner. In 1835 she took Emily's place at Roe Head, but became so ill that she had to be brought home to recover her health. From April to December 1839 she was governess at Blake Hall, Mirfield, finding like her sisters and so many other Victorian governesses that the children of large houses could be tyrannical monsters. In March 1841 she went to a new post with the Robinsons at Thorp Green and remained there more or less contentedly, with brief visits home, until Branwell's scandal obliged her to return to Haworth in 1845. On 28th May

1849 she died of consumption at Scarborough, having gone there with Charlotte and her friend Ellen Nussey in a last attempt to escape the fate that had recently claimed Branwell and Emily.

There was nothing remarkable in early Victorian times about these four short and melancholy lives, three of them lived in an atmosphere of restraint and dutifulness, all of them ending too early in painful deaths. What makes them perhaps the most remarkable family of the entire nineteenth century — and what brings those hundreds of thousands of visitors annually, many of them from as far afield as the United States and Japan — is the astonishing flowering of literary genius in the three sisters during the quiet hours of their childhoods, when they concocted, together with Branwell, the minutely written, hand-sewn booklets that chronicled the affairs of their imaginary realms of Angria and Gondal. These miniature epics of invention can be seen at the Parsonage Museum. As young adults, under the pseudonyms of Currer, Ellis and Acton Bell, the three sisters wrote six of the most celebrated novels ever published — novels which continue to sell in increasing numbers today. Charlotte's *Jane Eyre*, with its portrait of the independent-minded young governess and her long-drawn love for Mr Rochester, is considered by many readers to be the finest novel ever written, and contains many feminist ideas that shocked its audience when it was first published in October 1847. Her subsequent works maintained the same standard — *Shirley*, finished in the first agonies of loneliness and depression after the deaths of her brother and two sisters and published in October 1849, which brings in many recognizable local characters to the story's background of Luddite riots; and *Villette*, published in January 1853, whose heroine, Lucy Snowe, goes through much the same torments of love as Charlotte over Monsieur Heger, in a boarding school modelled largely on the Academy in Brussels. After this pinnacle of achievement, Charlotte did not take up her pen again in earnest until shortly before her death to write the first chapters of her unfinished last novel, *Emma*. In 1857 her first novel, *The Professor*, rejected many times in the period before *Jane Eyre*, finally saw the light of day.

The gentle Anne's output, *Agnes Grey* (December 1847)

and *The Tenant of Wildfell Hall* (July 1848) both treat in an understated, quietly heartfelt manner of courageous women in adversity — the governess and the long-suffering wife of a drunken husband. Her books, and those of Charlotte, however, brilliant crop from apparently barren soil as they are, lack the intense, almost demonic power and dramatic force of Emily's one towering masterpiece, *Wuthering Heights*. From Lockwood's meeting with Heathcliff on the opening page of the novel, the reader is dragged irresistibly into a story of a relentless will grinding mercilessly against the objects of both its love and hatred, crushing the weak and embracing the strong in a grip of doom. Around Catherine Earnshaw, Heathcliff and their victims are woven descriptions of the brooding, storm-ridden moors around Haworth where Emily walked in trances of communication with the natural world. This violent, closely detailed and often cruel book was the fruit of Emily's hard, fierce and inwardlooking genius—'. . . hewn in a wild workshop' as Charlotte wrote in her 1850 preface, 'with simple tools, and of homely materials. . . [the sculptor] wrought with a rude chisel, and from no model but the vision of his meditation.' From houses and places that she knew — Ponden Hall, the home of the Heaton family, friends of the Brontës; the isolated Top Withens farm, whose bleak position probably gave rise to Emily's description of the surroundings of Heathcliff's house, Wuthering Heights; High Sunderland near Law Hill where Emily was a governess in 1837, which resembled the description of the actual house of Wuthering Heights — Emily fashioned the background to the story developing in her fervent imagination during the long, peaceful writing sessions round the dining-room table at the Parsonage.

Haworth Parsonage is now a museum through whose doors pass a quarter of a million visitors a year. They can see Mr Brontë's pipe, spectacles and tobacco jar on the table in his study; the dining-room decorated in crimson, with the horse-hair sofa on which Emily coughed out her last hours; Mr Nicholls's green-papered study; the reconstructed kitchen where Tabitha Aykroyd spent most of her time with the infant Brontës; the neat, quiet bedrooms upstairs, with Brontë exhibits ranging from a plaited bracelet of Anne's hair to

Brontë Parsonage, Haworth

Charlotte's trim blue dress, Branwell's amateurish portraits and Emily's beautifully fierce water colour of her dog, Keeper, whose massive brass collar lies beside his portrait.

All is grave, silent, spotlessly clean and neat — Aunt Branwell wore wooden pattens for indoor cleanliness, whose clickings on the stone floors much amused the little Brontës. There is also a selection of foreign editions of *Wuthering Heights* — variously rendered as *De Woeste Hoogte*, *Les Hauts de Hurle-Vent* and *Hethuis in den Storm*. The museum also contains an enormous collection of Brontë manuscripts, letters and diaries.

It is hard to imagine the wild spirits of Heathcliff and Catherine raging through Emily's pen onto the paper in these small rooms — each about 15 feet square — while Agnes Grey and Jane Eyre took shape across the table. Our strenuous walk to the Brontë Bridge and Falls, a favourite resting-place of the sisters, to Top Withens and Ponden Hall, puts Emily's genius where it belongs — out on the moors where her untamed progeny had their birth.

* * *

The walk starts in the cobbled lane outside the Parsonage (029372) and passes the new extension behind the main building by a sign marked '*Haworth Moor*'. A path paved with flagstones hollowed by countless pilgrims' feet leads across the field — the way is often extremely muddy, and a pair of Aunt Branwell's pattens would not come amiss here. At the bottom corner of the field you join West Lane by a narrow stone stile, and fork left fifty yards up the road (024372). The route follows the tarmac road beneath a massive slab of rock engraved '*Penistone Hill Country Park*'. On the hillside to the left is Haworth Cemetery; on the right, the ridge-top village of Stanbury, where drystone field walls marking the boundaries of medieval strip fields curve in parallel lines above the flat waters of Lower Laithe Reservoir, built in 1925.

The road from Stanbury to Oxenhope is crossed (016365) at a green wooden sign, '*Public Footpath to Brontë Waterfalls $1\frac{1}{4}$*', beyond which a cattle-grid gives access to a tarred lane which winds past deserted farmhouses into open moorland, following a favourite walk of the Brontë sisters. The sodden peat-hags on the left of the lane, speckled with bright green sphagnum moss, disgorge water in a hundred streamlets, filling the air with the constant sound of trickling water which competes for the walker's attention in the solitude of the moors with the bleating of the tough black-faced sheep, the trilling of larks and the bubbling cry of curlews. The ruined farmhouses with their solid mullioned windows and barns built of a piece with the main living quarters bear silent witness to the harshness of conditions up here; the majority of the high moorland farmers have been forced down to lower levels by rain, wind, poor communications and poorer ground. The scenery loses its greenness, which is replaced by sombre browns and duns with splashes of purple heather in the summer months. The path, well defined but boggy after rain, changes from tarmac to yellow gravel, running on a ledge above a deep ravine on the right cut by the Sladen Beck through the gritstone. Stunted trees cling precariously to the falling hillside above the brown and peaty waters of the beck, which bubbles and twists among its rocks below the path. Emily Brontë's already inward-looking and intense imagination must have been fuelled by the stories of Tabitha

Aykroyd, which spoke of the fairies that sported at night over Sladen Beck. Their memory lingers on in the names of Hob Hill and Hob Lane, 'Hob' being a folk name for a fairy, goblin or devil.

The path descends to Brontë Bridge (998358), a clapper-bridge of millstone grit slabs across the beck. To the left up a narrow valley the Brontë Falls tumble in strings of white water from ledge to ledge down to their confluence with Sladen Beck; in high summer the falls dwindle to a meagre trickle, but after rain they swell to a cascade of broken curtains of water. There is a good view of the Falls from the Brontë Chair, a natural L-shaped seat in a sturdy slab of stone on the left of the path. Charlotte's association with this spot is sad. Newly pregnant, she accompanied her husband, the Reverend Arthur Bell Nicholls, on a walk to the Falls on 28th November 1854; but a soaking in a rainstorm on the way home led to a chill and subsequent fevers which culminated in her death on 31st March in the following year. The Falls and Bridge and the whole enclosing valley are small in scale, encompassed in an area of no more than three hundred yards. Quiet, remote, shut off from the outside world, it was a perfect haven for the Brontës. High up to the right, the blank-eyed ruins of Virginia Farm overlook the scene, reminiscent in their witness to human endeavour foiled by nature of the abandoned engine-houses and chimneys that dominate so many Cornish landscapes.

The path crosses Brontë Bridge and climbs steeply up the hillside through a gap in the wall to a signpost marked '*Withens*'. It slants upwards to traverse the ruins of another farmhouse and its field walls by stone stiles. Top Withens, the derelict farmhouse which was the site of Wuthering Heights, is now in view ahead, a dark blob with its two tattered trees just below the skyline (982355). In a blinding snowstorm across the cold shoulders of these hills ran Catherine Linton in Mr Lockwood's midnight vision in Chapter Three of the book, to beg for admittance to Wuthering Heights. Strange doings and violent passions seem natural to these elemental surroundings with their drab colours and hard outlines. Walking here, one can easily understand how a proud and fierce nature such as Emily's could have conceived the dark, dramatic loves and hatreds of her only adult novel.

The path crosses a stone wall by a set of slab steps and heads straight for Top Withens across the open moorland of Sandy Hill, very well defined and surfaced with tiny, sparkling chips of quartz from the underlying mill-stone grit. It descends to ford South Dean Beck (985356), along whose banks are the circular ruins of old sheep folds, and mounts up a peaty, muddy slope to the ruins of yet another abandoned farmhouse, where it joins the well-paved and distance-gobbling grand trunk route of walkers, the Pennine Way, which has come from Edale in Derbyshire and heads purposefully north-eastward for its eventual destination at Kirk Yetholm on the Scottish Border. Top Withens, or Wuthering Heights, lies a few hundred yards to the left on the Pennine Way, a squat, dark mass. Branwell Brontë mentions it under the name Darkwall and describes its 'large black walls and massy porch' as the subject of many a local fireside tale. Emily's description of her own creation is bleak and powerful:

> 'Wuthering Heights is the name of Mr Heathcliff's dwelling. "Wuthering" being a significant provincial adjective, descriptive of the atmospheric tumult to which its station is exposed in stormy weather. Pure, bracing ventilation they must have up there at all times, indeed: one may guess the power of the north wind, blowing over the edge, by the excessive slant of a few stunted firs at the end of the house; and by a range of gaunt thorns all stretching their limbs one way, as if craving alms of the sun. Happily, the architect had foresight to build it strong: the narrow windows are deeply set in the wall, and the corners defended with large jutting stones.'

The original substantial complex, half farmhouse and half barn, has been gradually eroded by weather and souvenir-hunters to a roofless, single-storey rectangle of truncated walls, whose crumbling stones have been capped with cement to prevent further decay. The farmhouse end is no more than a featureless ground-plan, the barn a rather better-preserved structure whose interior walls are built of mossy stones in tightly packed layers, their door and window openings outlined by stout stone lintels. Emily adorned the principal door of Wuthering Heights with 'a wilderness of crumbling griffins, and shameless little boys'. The western face of the barn, restored in larger blocks, contains a plaque placed there by the Brontë Society in 1964 recording the building's connection with Wuthering Heights, and pointing out that, even when inhabited, it bore no physical resemblance to the large dwelling described by Emily Brontë. However, its high and wild setting so near to Haworth, and its position in relation to Ponden Hall (believed to be the site of Thrushcross Grange, home of the Lintons in the novel), make it more than probable that Emily had the lonely farm in mind when she invented the Earnshaws' homestead where the demonic Heathcliff held sway. Here the young Catherine, as untameable as the curlews that cry over the nearby moors, conceived the passion for him that ruined her marriage to the mild Edgar Linton of Thrushcross Grange and drove her to her doom. Looking out across the superb views over Haworth, Keighley and Rombalds Moors, Emily stored up in her mind the windswept desolation of the scene which she would carry back with her to weave around Catherine and Heathcliff in the long quiet evenings at the Parsonage.

After admiring the view from the benches under the two gnarled trees (all that remain of the stocks, wallflowers and 'homely fruit trees' of Emily's description of the garden at Wuthering Heights), retrace your steps down the Pennine Way past its junction with the track up from South Dean Beck, and on beside Scar Hill, named after the black scree that marks the slipping of the hillside due to a fault-line at the base of the slope. The path crosses a beck by the stones of a derelict farmhouse, whose wall contains a curious cavity with an arched lintel — perhaps a bread oven or storage shelf. Great menhirs of stone gate-posts are incorporated into the wall that accompanies the path on the right, and the track dips up and down across the moor, trodden out by travellers to Top Withens and, more recently, by the boots of Pennine Way walkers on their 250-mile pilgrimage. Soon Ponden Reservoir appears far below. Just before Upper Heights Farm (992362) the path meets the right-angle of a wall on the left which dips sharply downhill towards the reservoir. Follow the wall down towards Far Slack Farm (992365) until it gives way to a wire-mesh fence. The farm is skirted to the right, the route crossing the drive and passing through a gate to continue downhill to a stone wall. Ignore the right-hand gap with a sheep-pass beside it, and take the rough opening to the left, dropping down to pass through a wooden wicket-gate on a strong spring. Immediately below is a newly restored farm building, which is again skirted to the right. This farm, known as Lower Slack, is being converted through a local youth scheme into an outdoor pursuits centre for activities based on Ponden Reservoir.

Straight ahead on the opposite slope is Ponden Hall, its grey stones blending with its surrounding trees and the hillside behind. As with Top Withens and Wuthering Heights, Emily Brontë took the situation of Ponden Hall and superimposed a building of her own invention, Thrushcross Grange. From Lower Slack the way is plain, down the hillside to a gate at the bottom which leads onto the pot-holed road round the reservoir. Turn left and climb a steep slope to reach the Hall (991372). The colourless Mr Lockwood, the narrator of the opening scene of *Wuthering Heights*, is the tenant of Thrushcross Grange, but it is Nellie Dean, his housekeeper, who brings alive the savage history of Heathcliff and Catherine and their bitter relationship with the gently bred and gently mannered Lintons who were the former inhabitants of the Grange. As children, Heathcliff and Cathy made a night-time expedition to the Grange and scared the wits out of Edgar Linton and his sister Isabella by peering in at them through the windows of the drawing-room. As adults, they broke the Lintons' hearts and lives, Heathcliff marrying Isabella and Catherine, Edgar; Isabella left Heathcliff, and Edgar's marriage to Catherine disintegrated when Heathcliff, after three years' absence, returned to Wuthering Heights. The offspring of these desperate unions, Heathcliff and Isabella's sickly son, Linton, and Cathy and Edgar's daughter, Catherine, were eventually coerced into a short-lived marriage with each other by the relentless Heathcliff, who had also managed to shatter the lives of his Catherine's brother, Hindley, and Hindley's son, Hareton. Round Thrushcross Grange was woven a web of hatred and revenge that trapped its hapless inmates and ruined them one by one. Somehow the parson's daughter from Haworth contrived to build this remorseless, intense and vivid story from the resources of her

131

own imagination and the wild surroundings of her home.

The present-day Ponden Hall is rather happier — a friendly house where bed-and-breakfasters are greeted by fires, dogs, home-brewed beer and good food; where the owner weaves tapestries at a hand-loom, and the walls of the dark-beamed drawing-room are hung with modern pictures as well as solemn portraits of Victorian businessmen; where informality and cheerfulness are the key-notes. The house's history is neatly summed up in a plaque above the main door: '*The Old houfe now Standing was built by Robert Heaton for his Son Michael Anno Domini 1634. The old Porch and Pea houfe was built by his Grandfon Robert Heaton A.D. 1680. The prefent Building was Rebuilt by his defcendant R.H. 1801.*'

The massive, low house is built of stone blocks, blotched with lichen; the garden is protected from the biting local winds by a high stone wall.

From Ponden Hall, the path leads back to the field gate and along the edge of Ponden Reservoir to the dam wall at the eastern end. Here it continues straight on between low stone walls to meet the Stanbury road (000373) at Ponden Mill; built in the 1790s and the oldest mill still standing in the Worth Valley, it has recently taken on a new lease of life as a craft and textile centre.

The road to Stanbury climbs steeply uphill. Set into the right-hand wall are a stone water-trough for yesterday's means of transport, and a grit container for today's! This road can be congested and unpleasant at the height of the tourist season, but Stanbury is worth the climb — a long, dark, typical Yorkshire ridge village, its sombre houses set closely along the road, its school adorned with a forbidding notice about use of the playground after school hours, its church a blunt, uncompromising block crouched under gloomy trees. In the church is a pulpit, from Haworth Old Church, from which Mr Brontë preached many a sermon. Suddenly, at the end of the village, the view opens out, and there are Oakworth and Haworth ahead among the valley slopes, light after dark, and space after enclosure, a perfect example of the characteristic West Riding contrast of landscape.

After leaving the village you turn right at a sign '*Worth Valley Railway. Oxenhope 2*' (013372), and drop downhill to cross the Lower Laithe Reservoir by the dam wall. Bear left at the end of the wall, (015368) and walk up a tarmac track above the Sladen Valley water-treatment plant which soon turns into a rough path that climbs to join the Haworth road under the cemetery. From here you follow the road to West Lane and the field path back to the Parsonage Museum, taking with you some of Emily Brontë's visions of Heathcliff, Catherine and the lonely outpost of Wuthering Heights.

The Brontë Society
c/o The Hon. Secretary, The Brontë Parsonage, Haworth, Keighley, West Yorks BD22 8DR (Tel: Haworth (0535) 42323)
Established in 1893 'to bring closer together all who honoured the Brontë sisters'. The Society runs the Brontë Parsonage Museum (open all year round except the last three weeks in December). Its 'Transactions' are published annually. Research in the Society's library is permitted by prior arrangement.

Local library
The North-West Area Library, North Street, Keighley, West Yorks BD21 3SX

Useful books
There is an immense amount of biographical and critical material on the Brontë sisters. Particularly useful are:
Transactions of the Brontë Society (see above)
Life of Charlotte Brontë by Elizabeth Gaskell. Published 1857
The Brontë Story by Margaret Lane. Published by Heinemann, 1953 and Fontana Books, 1969
The Brontës and their World by Phyllis Bentley. Published by Thames & Hudson, 1969
Haworth and the Brontës — a visitor's guide by W.R. Mitchell. Published by Dalesman, 1967

Round Grasmere and Rydal Water with Dorothy Wordsworth

Home at Grasmere — Extracts from the Journal of Dorothy Wordsworth and from the poems of William Wordsworth
edited by Colette Clark
Penguin paperback, 1978

(Dove Cottage — Nab Scar — Rydal Mount — Steps End — Loughrigg Terrace — Red Bank Wood — Allan Bank — Grasmere Church — Dove Cottage. About six miles by lanes and hilly footpaths. Gentle climbs — no fell-walking gear needed)

O.S.– 1:50,000 Sheet No. 90 'Penrith, Keswick and Ambleside'
1:25,000 Outdoor Leisure Map — 'The English Lakes (South-East): Windermere and Kendal'

' . . . the calmest, fairest spot on earth
My own; and not mine only, for with me
Entrenched, say rather peacefully embowered,
Under yon orchard, in yon humble cot,
A younger Orphan of a home extinct,
The only Daughter of my Parents dwells.
            . . . Mine eyes did ne'er
Fix on a lovely object, nor my mind
Take pleasure in the midst of happy thoughts,
But either She whom now I have, who now
Divides with me this loved abode, was there,
Or not far off. Where'er my footsteps turned,
Her voice was like a hidden Bird that sang.
The thought of her was like a flash of light,
Or an unseen companionship, a breath
Of fragrance independent of the wind . . .'
            ('The Recluse' — Book First: 'Home at Grasmere')

Opposite: *Dorothy Wordsworth, a portrait painted by S. Crosthwaite in 1833, just before the onset of her long illness*

Dorothy Wordsworth was nearly thirty years old when her brother William wrote these tender lines about her. The 'calmest, fairest spot on earth' was Grasmere Vale, where brother and sister had recently come to live; and 'yon humble cot' the little cottage at Town-End, now known to the world as Dove Cottage. Here for eight blissful years they led their lives totally wrapped up in each other and in the beauties of Grasmere, walking, gardening, entertaining friends and developing their philosophy of 'plain living and high thinking'. They shared everything in those golden years, during which Dorothy transcribed the flood of exquisite poems that poured out of William in response to the wild splendour of the Lakeland hills and valleys — poems that were often inspired by her own powers of observation. 'My love for my brother', she wrote, 'was the building up of my being, the light of my path.'

Dorothy was born on Christmas Eve 1771, in Cockermouth, a little coastal town on the north-west border of the Lake District. She was the third child of John Wordsworth, an attorney-at-law employed as agent by Sir James Lowther, the chief local landowner. Dorothy's brother William had been born on 7th April the previous year, and grew up a wild, tempestuous boy. He and Dorothy were very close even as young children, and William found a measure of stability in his love for the sensitive, highly-strung sister whose gentle appreciation of nature complemented his enthusiasm:

> 'Oh! pleasant, pleasant were the days,
> The time, when in our childish plays,
> My sister Emmeline and I
> Together chased the butterfly!
> A very hunter did I rush
> Upon the prey:- with leaps and springs
> I followed on from brake to bush;
> But she, God love her! feared to brush
> The dust from off its wings.'
> ('To a Butterfly')

After the death of their mother in 1778, Dorothy was sent to live with relations in Halifax, Yorkshire, while William went the following year to Hawkshead Grammar School between Windermere and Coniston. Although Dorothy's relations were kind to her, she sadly missed the brother who was spending his time roaming over the fells in all weathers and at all times of day and night. Nine years passed before their reunion in 1787, but the long separation only strengthened the bond between brother and sister. 'William and Christopher' — her youngest brother — 'are very clever boys,' she wrote to a friend, 'at least so they appear in the partial eyes of a Sister. No doubt I am partial and see virtues in them that by everybody else will pass unnoticed.'

Their father had died in 1783, his estate largely in the form of unpaid debts, and the recovery of this money (most of it owed by Sir James Lowther) preoccupied the hard-up Wordsworth children for the next twenty years. William went to Cambridge in 1787, where he worked hard for the first year and then became disillusioned with University life, just about scraping his degree in 1791. Meanwhile Dorothy was left with more relations at Penrith, trying to cope with 'the ill-nature of my Grandfather and Uncle Christopher'. In 1789 her Uncle William brought her south to Norfolk for a happier period as his housekeeper. She established classes for local poor children, and became friendly with William Wilberforce. The friendship never developed into a romance, however — Dorothy was dedicated to her brother, and was already making plans for a future life with him in some solitary refuge of nature and plain living.

William made two trips to the Continent during his time at Cambridge, the first in 1790 when he was deeply affected by the revolutionary fervour in France — the Bastille had been stormed the year before. His second trip in 1791–2 was even more eventful, for he had a passionate love affair with Annette Vallon, a 25-year-old Frenchwoman, and by Christmas 1792 was the father of a daughter, Caroline. Back in England, William told Dorothy all about it; and she gave him complete support, to the extent of writing his letters to Annette for him. William fully intended to marry his lover, but war was declared in 1793 before he could return to France. The war dragged on until 1802, by which time he was engaged to be married to a childhood sweetheart, Mary Hutchinson.

Uncle William, when the news of William's affair reached him, forbade Dorothy to see her brother, or even to talk about him. Such a strong-willed and independent young lady would not meekly accept this excommunication. She met William secretly in Halifax, the old plans for a romantic life together were resurrected, and in spring 1794 they escaped to Windy Brow Farm near Keswick for two delightful months together. When the money ran out Dorothy returned to relations at Barrow, but then William was left £900 by his friend Raisley Calvert of Windy Brow. In 1795 he and Dorothy moved to the West Country — first to Dorset, then to the Quantock Hills. Here they made friends with Robert Southey — himself a future Poet Laureate but at that time a struggling young poet — and with Samuel Taylor Coleridge, who was to remain their closest friend for the next ten years.

In 1795 there were no shadows in Coleridge of the opium-crazed, overweight hypochondriac he later became. A vigorous, energetic and optimistic youth, he, Dorothy and William soon formed a seemingly inseparable unit. His description of Dorothy at that time is full of affection:

> 'If you expected to see a pretty woman, you would think her ordinary; if you expected to see an ordinary woman, you would think her pretty, but her manners were simple, ardent, impressive. In every motion, her most innocent soul outbeams so brightly that who saw her would say, guilt was a thing impossible to her.'

To raise money, Coleridge and William put their heads together to compile a book of poems. *Lyrical Ballads* came out in September 1798 while the three of them were away in Germany; but it was not an immediate critical or financial success. The style of the poems was radically new, as was their content. There was no idealizing of nature, no convoluted verse forms, no following of conventional rules. Here were two young poets writing in a straightforward manner about things they actually saw, about crippled and mad people, about ordinary folk living their daily lives, and about the unadorned appearance of nature. 'The Thorn' received a good deal of criticism for its simplicity and matter-of-fact style:

> 'There is a Thorn — it looks so old,
> In truth, you'd find it hard to say
> How it could ever have been young,

It looks so old and grey.
Not higher than a two year's child
It stands erect, this aged Thorn;
No leaves it has, no prickly points;
It is a mass of knotted joints,
A wretched thing forlorn.
It stands erect, and like a stone
With lichens is it overgrown.'

The book contains two poems nowadays acknowledged as masterpieces — Coleridge's 'The Rime of the Ancient Mariner', and Wordsworth's 'Lines composed a few Miles above Tintern Abbey'.

Back in England in 1799 and still chronically short of money, William went on a walking tour of the Lakes with his younger brother, John. The Lake District had been the delight of poets and painters for at least one hundred years; and William, looking for the first time at the little cottage at the foot of Grasmere Vale, began to consider settling down there. The cottage had been an inn, the Dove and Olive Bough, but was now available for new tenants. On 20th December 1799, William and Dorothy moved in.

Dorothy quickly furnished the little house and settled down to her life of baking, sewing, ironing, cooking, cleaning, gardening and copying out William's poems. There was almost no wheeled traffic in the district at that date, so in spite of the fact that the road passed their front door they lived in a silence and tranquillity unimaginable nowadays. They fashioned a lovely garden out of the steep hillside behind the house, went walking round the twin lakes of Grasmere and Rydal Water ('Rydale' as Dorothy always called it) and up the surrounding fells, and received a constant stream of guests, many of whom stayed on for weeks or months, camping out in the cramped cottage and sharing the Wordsworths' frugal meals of porridge and home-grown vegetables. Coleridge came in April 1800, and liked the area so much that he moved his family north to a house which Dorothy found for him, Greta Hall near Keswick. Coleridge often left his wife and children to stay with William and Dorothy; by now he was addicted to laudanum, that deadly opium-based pain-killer which hooked so many unsuspecting victims, and frequently spent days in bed, prostrated with nerves and sickness. Dorothy's love for him was mixed with worry, as she revealed on 10th November 1801 in the Journal she had begun the previous year:

'Every sight and every sound reminded me of him — dear, dear fellow, of his many walks to us by day and by night, of all dear things. I was melancholy, and could not talk, but at last I eased my heart by weeping — nervous blubbering, says William. It is not so. O! how many, many reasons have I to be anxious for him.'

Dorothy kept her Journal faithfully from 14th May 1800 to 16th January 1803, partly at William's request to refresh his memory over possible subjects for poems, partly to give expression to her own creative talent. She always regretted that she could not compose poetry, but some of the passages in the Journal have a simple poetical quality that rings out:

23rd March 1802: 'It is about 10 o'clock, a quiet night. The fire flutters, and the watch ticks. I hear nothing else save the breathing of my Beloved, and he now and then pushes his book forward, and turns over a leaf.'

Her descriptions of their walks together glow with appreciation of the beauty of nature. This passage might have been penned by Francis Kilvert:

12th December 1801: 'The moon shone upon the water below Silver-How, and above it hung, combining with Silver-How on one side, a bowl-shaped moon, the curve downwards; the white fields, glittering roof of Thomas Ashburner's house, the dark yew tree, the white fields gay and beautiful. Wm. lay with his curtains open that he might see it.'

In this intense, happy time most of William's best verse was composed. On 11th March 1802 he worked at 'The Singing Bird'; on 12th March he finished it and began 'Alice Fell'; on 13th he finished 'Alice Fell' and wrote most of 'Beggars'; on 14th he finished 'Beggars' before breakfast — 'and while we were at breakfast. . . with his basin of broth before him untouched, and a little plate of bread and butter, he wrote the Poem to a Butterfly! He ate not a morsel nor put on his stockings, but sate with his shirt neck unbuttoned, and his waist coat open while he did it.'

Dorothy had been the source of inspiration for that poem, as she was for many other verses, lines or whole poems.

The intensity of Dorothy's feelings for William made her over-anxious about his health:

> *4th Nov. 1800* — 'Wm. sadly tired — threatenings of the piles.'
> *5th Nov.* — 'Wm. not well.'
> *6th Nov.* — 'Wm. somewhat better.'
> *7th Nov.* — 'Wm. still unwell.'
> *26th Nov.* — 'Wm. very well, and highly poetical.'

In fact, William and Dorothy were both tough people, who thought nothing of walking fifteen or twenty miles.

The balance of their relationship had to change, albeit slowly, when William married his sweetheart Mary Hutchinson on 4th October 1802. Dorothy was overcome with emotion on the wedding day and could not bring herself to go to church for the marriage ceremony. She went with the happy couple on their honeymoon, which ended cosily enough with Dorothy cradling William on her breast in the post-chaise while she slept on Mary's shoulder. Dorothy and Mary were genuinely fond of each other, but as William's love for his wife grew in intensity with the passing years, so his special relationship with Dorothy lost its ardour. While Mary was pregnant with, or nursing, the five children that she bore William between 1803 and 1810, he still relied on Dorothy for his emotional nourishment; but once Mary was free of the demands of the nursery she began to take Dorothy's place nearest to William's heart. Dorothy seems to have understood and come to terms with the changed situation; but she ceased writing her Journal on a daily basis only three months after the wedding.

Many other changes had taken place to disturb the tranquillity of life at Town-End by the time they left it in 1808. *Lyrical Ballads* had begun to bring in some money, boosting William's annual income to about £80. Coleridge, raddled by opium addiction and depression, left England in January 1804 to try to recover his health on a long tour of the Mediterranean.

He left his three precocious children in the care of his wife and of Dorothy, who transferred to them much of the love that had hitherto been William's alone.

In 1805 brother John went down with his ship *The Earl of Abergavenny* in a storm off Portland Bill. His death devastated the Wordsworth household, which was further upset by the terrible change in Coleridge that they all saw when he returned to England in 1806. Overweight and puffy, his appearance appalled Dorothy:

> '. . . that he is ill I am well assured, and must sink if he does not grow more happy. His fatness has quite changed him — it is more like the flesh of a person in dropsy than one in health; his eyes are lost in it . . .'

William's *Poems in Two Volumes* came out in 1807. It was savagely attacked by the reviewers, although it contained a number of the poems by which he is best known today — 'I Wandered Lonely as a Cloud', 'To the Daisy', 'Composed upon Westminster Bridge, September 3, 1802', 'The Rainbow', and many others.

In 1807 the shy, 21-year-old Thomas De Quincey finally nerved himself to meet William, whom he had long admired. De Quincey, whose *Confessions of an Opium-Eater* brought him notoriety when it was published in 1821, recorded his first impressions of Town-End: 'a little white cottage gleaming from the midst of trees.' He, too, made a long stay, though he was never as intimate with the Wordsworths as Coleridge had been. De Quincey's description of Dorothy highlights the untamed quality of her character:

> 'Her face was of Egyptian brown . . . Her eyes were not soft as Mrs Wordsworth's, nor were they fierce or bold, but they were wild and startling, and hurried in their motion. Her utterance and enunciation generally suffered in point of clearness from the agitation of her excessive sensibility.'

By May 1808 the ménage at Town-End, comprising William, Mary, Dorothy, Mary's sister Sarah, Coleridge, De Quincey and the three children already born to William and

Mary — and a fourth one on the way — threatened to burst the walls of the little cottage. Allan Bank, a large house newly built under Silver Howe at the western end of Grasmere, was available, and they moved there lock, stock and barrel. De Quincey soon took over Town-End and kept the tenancy for the next twenty-eight years. He had seven children and a library of five thousand books, so space was just as constricted as when the Wordsworths lived there. Like Coleridge, De Quincey succumbed to the lure of opium, at one stage regularly taking between 8,000 and 12,000 drops of laundanum a day — three or four times the lethal dose.

Allan Bank proved a bad choice, and its smoky fires and many other uncomfortable features drove the Wordsworths out to the Rectory in Grasmere in 1811. By now there were five children, though the damp and cold of the Rectory soon accounted for two of them — little Catherine and Thomas dying within six months of each other. Dorothy hated the Rectory: 'The house only reminded me of desolate gloom, emptiness, and cheerless silence.'

By contrast, the next house (and their last) was 'a paradise . . . the nicest place in the world for children.' In 1813 they moved to Rydal Mount, a large, secluded old farmhouse overlooking the eastern end of Rydal Water, with a spacious garden soon improved and extended by William. The same regime of frugal meals and long walks was kept up by the household; but by now William had become a famous man, to be visited by other famous or would-be famous tourists in the Lakes. (The youthful John Keats called in 1818, but William happened to be out and the two did not meet.) Financial worries were banished in 1813 when William was appointed Distributor of Stamps for Westmorland through the good offices of William Lowther, now Lord Lonsdale, who had paid off his family's debts to the Wordsworths ten years before; the job brought in an extra £200 a year. As William's marriage brought him greater peace of mind, so his political views changed, until by the 1820s, now an established 'great man' since the publication of his River Duddon sonnets, he was as reactionary a supporter of the status quo as any landed gentleman. He became friendly with the family of Dr Thomas Arnold — the famous Arnold of Rugby of *Tom Brown's*

Schooldays — who had a house at Fox Howe nearby, and he saw a good deal of Robert Southey, now Poet Laureate.

Dorothy, meanwhile, took to going away from Rydal Mount for months at a time to help look after the children of her friends and relations. She still corresponded with Annette Vallon and Caroline, and in 1820 went with William to France for a reunion with his erstwhile lover and their daughter. Dora, William's daughter by Mary, grew up a strong-willed young lady who pushed her aunt further and further into the background of William's affections. In 1829 Dorothy nearly died of 'internal inflammation'. She recovered, but the effects of the illness kept her a partial invalid; and by 1835 she had become mentally unstable. Twenty twilight years followed, of wheelchairs and psychological decay, interspersed with lucid periods in which she would recite William's verses faultlessly.

Poor Coleridge, for many years *persona non grata* in the Wordsworth household, had died in 1834. In the following years Dora married and died of consumption; Coleridge's son Hartley — like Branwell Brontë, never fulfilling his early promise — died young; and William became Poet Laureate after Southey's death in 1843.

On Tuesday, 23rd April 1850 William died, full of years and honours. His devoted Dorothy followed him in January 1855, at the age of eighty-three.

> 'The Blessing of my later years
> Was with me when a boy:
> She gave me eyes, she gave me ears;
> And humble cares, and delicate fears;
> A heart, the fountain of sweet tears;
> And love, and thought, and joy.'
>   (From 'The Sparrow's Nest' —
>   composed at Town-End, 1801)

*   *   *

Dove Cottage (342070) stands with its neighbouring bookshop and Wordsworth Museum in the lane that was once the main road from Grasmere to Rydal. A diminutive house with a whitewashed, rough-cast exterior up which the roses planted by William and Dorothy still grow, its interior is dark and unadorned, a series of small, simply furnished rooms with low ceilings and dark panelling. Diamond-paned windows and stone-flagged floors (covered with rushes in the Wordsworths' day) complete the picture of rustic plainness.

There was a bed in every room when guests came to stay — all except for the damp little cellarage off the kitchen, known as the Buttery, where the Dove and Olive Bough kept its beer cool. Coleridge would sleep in the sitting-room and the latest baby in a basket under the kitchen sink. Sir Walter Scott so disliked the Wordsworths' humble meals of 'paritch' — and he a Scotsman! — that he climbed out of his bedroom window into the garden early one morning and sneaked off to the Swan for a square breakfast. From William's study upstairs the poet could enjoy an uninterrupted view across the green fields to Grasmere Lake and Silver Howe rising majestically from the opposite shore. Houses have been built since 1800 between Dove Cottage and the lake, blocking off this much-loved view.

On the walls of the cottage are many pictures of the Wordsworth circle, including a very lively drawing of De Quincey in middle age with a ravaged, ascetic face and visionary's eyes that glow out of the frame. William's passport for his trip in 1837 to Italy during which he met his daughter Caroline for the last time — it hangs in his bedroom — is a good factual yardstick by which to measure the numerous portraits of him:

Height: 5ft 9½ins	Eyes: Grey
Age: 66 years	Nose: Medium
Hair: Greying	Chin: Round
Forehead: Bald	Face: Oval
Eyebrows: White	Complexion: Ordinary

Behind the house the garden rises steeply up the bank, its flagged walks as neat as the day William laid them. At the top is a summer house, near the spot where Dorothy planned to build 'a seat with a summer shed on the highest platform in this our little domestic slip of mountain. The spot commands a view over the roof of our house, of the lake, the church, Helm Cragg, and two thirds of the vale' (William's letter to Coleridge, Christmas Eve 1799). Nowadays, as noted above, the houses in front of Dove Cottage cut off most of this charming view.

The Museum beside the house contains a beautifully laid-out exhibition, taking the visitor through the Wordsworth story in chronological order.

Facing Dove Cottage from the road, turn right and walk up the lane to How Top Farm on the right. In the woods above the lane William often walked, composing and revising his verses. Opposite How Top Farm take the track on the left marked *No Through Road for Motors* and *Route to Rydal* (343068), that climbs between bracken banks from which jut crags of bare rock. The path levels out in an avenue of saplings, and soon emerges with a view down to the right of the western end of Rydal Water. Drystone walls enclose the rough track, which runs between ash and oak trees under the sheer, stony face of Nab Scar, whose rocky outcrops tower above. The crinkled crags of Loughrigg Fell overlook Rydal Water away to the right.

The path becomes narrow, more stony and steeper, passing through a succession of gates, mounting and falling over stones smoothed by generations of walkers' feet. The incessant roar of traffic on the A591 Ambleside—Grasmere road does not quite drown out the mew of buzzards and occasional 'cronk' of a raven flying down the valley. Dorothy, William and Coleridge came here on 23rd April 1802.

'We determined to go under Nab Scar. Thither we went. The sun shone and we were lazy. Coleridge pitched upon several places to sit down upon, but we could not be all of one mind respecting sun and shade, so we pushed on to the foot of the scar. It was very grand when we looked up, very stony, here and there a budding tree . . .'

Coleridge soon found a hidden place high up in the face of the scar: 'the sweetest ever seen. . . about this bower there is mountain-ash, common-ash, yew-tree, ivy, holly, hawthorn, mosses and flowers, and a carpet of moss.'

In the lane under the scar on 1st December 1801 Dorothy and Mary Hutchinson were overtaken by two drunken soldiers who were 'very merry and very civil. They fought with the mountains with their sticks. "Aye," says one, "that will fall upon us. One might stride over that, etc."'

As you leave the woods there is a view down to the right of Heron Island and Little Isle in Rydal Water, side by side. Rydal Water, 'soft, chearful and beautiful', was one of Dorothy's favourite places, and one she never tired of describing:

> *2nd June 1800*: 'The waves round about the little Island seemed like a dance of spirits that rose out of the water, round its small circumference of shore.'

October 19th in the same year was a misty day, which showed off the calm subtlety of the shapes and colours to their best advantage:

> 'Rydal was very, very beautiful. The surface of the water quite still, like a dim mirror. The colours of the large island exquisitely beautiful, and the trees still fresh and green were magnified by the mists. . .'

At its deepest part Rydal Water is sixty feet deep. When it freezes over in winter intrepid local people still bring their skates here, at risk of a ducking or worse, as William loved to do.

Below the path the roofs of Nab Cottage shelter under the hillside (355064). In 1816 De Quincey had an affair with the farmer's daughter, Margaret Simpson, and she became pregnant. The following year she married him — a happy and successful marriage, in spite of De Quincey's subsequent decline. In 1849 Hartley Coleridge, the wayward son of the Wordsworths' old friend, died in an upstairs room at Nab Cottage. In the face of Loughrigg Fell on the opposite shore of the lake is the great dark mouth of a disused quarry.

As you walk towards Rydal village, the view ahead is dominated by the enormous dun-coloured shoulder of Wansfell, criss-crossed by the thin lines of drystone walls. The path descends towards the village, becoming a tarmac lane before emerging above the grey walls, irregular roofs and chimney stacks of Rydal Mount (363064), the Wordsworths' home from 1813 onwards. The large and lovely gardens, most of their paths and terraces laid out by William, look out over the lake to the rising wall of Lanty Scar, girdled with conifers. The neatly clipped lawns and well-stocked flower beds give way to grassy terraces and flights of steps running up and down the slope of the hill. At the top of the garden, as at Dove Cottage, is a summer house, perfectly placed among the trees for solitude and meditation. Thank goodness William never experienced the rash assault of the gear-changing traffic on the A591 below, or the scream of low-flying jets overhead!

The house is large and imposing, but still in scale with the Wordsworthian 'plain living' philosophy. William, Mary and Dorothy enjoyed the extra space compared with tiny Town-End, and the freedom from smoky chimneys and damp rooms that had spoiled Allan Bank and Grasmere Rectory. Their furniture, while mostly second-hand, was finer than that at Town-End, the pictures by more celebrated artists, and the visitors more exalted — Queen Adelaide, the widow of King William IV, paid a visit in 1840. In the library hangs a portrait of Dorothy at the age of sixty-one, painted in 1833 by S. Crosthwaite. It shows a heavy-faced woman with a rather pinched and down-turned mouth, a determined chin, and copious golden hair escaping from her frilly bonnet. The eyes are deep-set, grey and direct — the Dorothy of the Journal lives on in them, though the rest of the face is marked by introspection and illness.

From Rydal Mount walk down the lane past Rydal Church with its castellated tower and Victorian Gothic windows. It was opened on Christmas Day 1824, William having helped to choose the site, and soon numbered the Wordsworths and the Arnolds from Fox Howe among its worshippers. Behind the church is the Rashfield, so called because of the rushes which grew there, now usually known as Dora's Field in memory of William's dearest child, to whom he gave it.

Cross the A591 and turn right. In fifty yards turn off left opposite the Glen Rothay Hotel to cross the peaty brown River Rothay by a wooden footbridge (363062). On the far bank turn right and follow a well-defined track by the river, from which the full majesty of Nab Scar can be appreciated. Ahead the 'tall steep of Silver-How' closes the valley at the

Grasmere end. The path goes through a kissing-gate — bear immediately left up the hillside at 30°, taking the middle of three paths (359060), and enter Rydal Woods, keeping straight ahead to reach the old quarries. First comes an excavation in the rock-face to the left of the path, guarded by a romantic crag; then you come to the main delving, a great waterlogged echoing cavern at the end of a ledge of mining spoil. From here the path drops down, then up again to the left above the lake onto Loughrigg Terrace.

Dorothy wrote on 1st June 1800: 'I lay upon the steep of Loughrigg, my heart dissolved in what I saw. . .' and it really is a heart-dissolving view (345058) over the full extent of Grasmere to the church and village at the far end, and beyond to the road winding over Dunmail Raise. All around are the hills — in the left foreground the upthrust escarpment of Helm Crag; behind it the green shoulder of Steel Fell, which sweeps in a long curve down to Dunmail Raise and up the other side to Seat Sandal, a backdrop for Great Rigg Man and Heron Pike. Framed in the sweep of Steel Fell and Seat Sandal is the irregular hump of Lonscale Fell, 2,344 feet high and nearly twenty miles away.

Dorothy described the view on Boxing Day 1801:

'Grasmere Lake a beautiful image of stillness, clear as glass, reflecting all things, the wind was up, and the waters sounding. The lake of a rich purple, the fields of soft yellow, the island yellowish-green, the copses red-brown, the mountains purple. The Church and buildings, how quiet they were!'

The view from Loughrigg Terrace inspired one of William's most beautiful passages in 'The Excursion':

'The Valley, opening out her bosom, gave
Fair prospect, intercepted less and less,
O'er the flat meadows and indented coast
Of the smooth lake, in compass seen: — far off,
And yet conspicuous, stood the old church-tower,
In majesty presiding over fields
And habitations seemingly preserved
From all intrusion of the restless world
By rocks impassable and mountains huge . . .'
(Ninth Book, lines 571 – 579)

On the island in the middle of the lake can be seen a stone building, once a sheep-pen. William often went there to think and compose. A more impious visitor was Edward VII when Prince of Wales, who with a companion chased the sheep and was roundly ticked off by the old woman who owned them for a 'badly browt-up barn o' somebody's'.

When you have gazed your fill, carry on through a kissing-gate, keeping left between walls through the wood, then bearing right at a fork in the path to join a minor road (340057). Turn right along the road, ignoring the path immediately opposite, and in one hundred yards take the next track on the left which leads through Red Bank Woods. At a kissing-gate at the end of the wood (336060) turn down to your right on a stony track from which there are fine views over the lake as you descend to join a tarmac road at Huntingstile (333064). The high ridge which connects Great Rigg Man, Heron Pike and Nab Scar is now in full view on your right. Continue along the road for about a mile, beguiling the way by admiring the splendid horse chestnuts, sycamores, beech, silver birch and oaks which line the road.

As you near the main road, Allan Bank is situated ahead on a raised piece of ground backed by trees and the pointed top of Helm Crag, which is known locally as the Lion and Lamb, Hen and Chickens and, rather enigmatically, the Lady playing an Organ.

Now make for the square tower of Grasmere's Church of St Oswald in the centre of the village.

'Not raised in nice proportion was the Pile
But large and massy, for duration built
With pillars crowded, and the roof upheld
By naked rafters intricately crossed.'

William's often-quoted description still holds good today. On the Saturday nearest St Oswald's Day (5th August) the residents of Grasmere perform the ancient rush-bearing ceremony, a procession carrying rushes to the church. In times past these were strewn on the floor as a kind of primitive central heating and to mask the floor of beaten earth that William and Dorothy knew.

Before walking the last half-mile back to Dove Cottage, go through the churchyard gate and take the path to the left to find the Wordsworth family graves. William and Mary lie together, their plain headstones recording simply their names. Dorothy lies beside them, inseparable in death as in life.

The Grasmere & Wordsworth Museum
Dove Cottage, Town End, Grasmere, Cumbria LA22 9SG (Tel: Grasmere (09665) 544). Open March, April—September, October. The Dove Cottage Trust was founded in 1890 to secure 'the eternal possession' of Dove Cottage for 'all those who love English poetry all over the world'.
Dove Cottage, the Museum, the new Wordsworth Research Library (still to be completed) and the Bookshop form the Wordsworth Heritage Centre.

Useful books
A selection from the mass of literature available:
Guide to the Lakes by William Wordsworth, edited by Ernest de Sélincourt. Published in paperback by Oxford University Press, 1977
William Wordsworth by Hunter Davies. Published in paperback by Hamlyn, 1981
A Walk around the Lakes by Hunter Davies. Published in paperback by Hamlyn, 1980
Grasmere and the Wordsworths — a tourist's guide by W.R. Mitchell. Published by Dalesman, 1970
The Wordsworth Poetical Guide to the Lakes by Richard J. Hutchings. Published by Hunnyhill Publications (Corner Cottage, Hunnyhill, Brighstone, Isle of Wight), 1977
Grasmere — A Short History compiled by members of Grasmere Women's Institute (edited by Rachel Macalpine). Published by Titus Wilson (Kendal), 1979
Grasmere in Wordsworth's Time by Eleanor F. Rawnsley. Published by Titus Wilson (Kendal)

A Walk with the Pitman Poet

ANTHOLOGIES
Come All Ye Bold Miners — ballads and songs of the coalfields, compiled by A.L. Lloyd. Lawrence and Wishart Ltd
One Hundred Songs of Toil compiled and edited by Karl Dallas. Wolfe Publishing
Tommy Armstrong Sings edited by Tom Gilfellon. Frank Graham

RECORDS
'The Bonnie Pit Laddie' and 'Tommy Armstrong of Tyneside', both by The High Level Ranters on Topic Records

(Beamish Open-Air Museum — Red Row — Tanfield Wagonway — Oakey's Pit — Stanley — Burn's Pit — Beamish. About six and a half miles through the mining villages of north-west Durham, by field paths, disused wagonway and minor roads. Allow three hours for the walk, leaving yourself plenty of time to stop and chat with local people about the area's history.)

O.S.– 1:50,000 Sheet No. 88 'Tyneside'
1:25,000 Sheets Nos. NZ 25/35 'Chester-le-Street' and NZ 15 'Consett (East)'

Whilst there is an embarrassment of literary riches to choose from in other parts of the country, the north-east of England is a different case. Here are fine far-flung panoramas from ridge-top viewpoints over twenty or thirty miles of rolling countryside around Durham, many acres of solitary moorland in Weardale and Teesdale, and mile upon mile of Northumbrian coastal scenery virtually untouched by the wheels of tourists. But life in this remote corner of Britain has

Opposite: *Tommy Armstrong (seated) outside the pub with his mates — note the notorious stick!*

been so hard for ordinary men and women through the centuries that few of them have set to with pen and paper to celebrate their native landscape. The wind-bitten sheep farms of Northumberland and the dales of Wear and Tees, the strength-sapping hard graft of docks and shipyards at the mouth of the river Tyne and dusty sweated labour of the coal pits demanded all the time and energy of their workers, most of whom until fifty years ago were at work before they had had any proper schooling. No Henry Williamsons came to Northumberland to write with an outsider's detachment of the people and countryside; no Wordsworth set down Weardale in imperishable verse; no Kilverts or Woodfordes recorded the day-to-day doings of the inhabitants of Shotton Colliery or Consett.

In songs and music, however, ill-educated and hard-worked people everywhere could express their thoughts and feelings on the local scene as clearly and imaginatively as the poets and diarists scribbling away in Grasmere, Clyro and Weston Longville. This musical and singing tradition was particularly strong in the north-east, and remains so today. Fiddlers, whistlers, concertina players and Northumbrian pipers are still sure of an enthusiastic audience in Newcastle pubs or rural back kitchens; and the old songs of sheep-shearing, herring-fishing and coal-mining have stayed alive. This area, now struggling against the hopelessness of long-term unemployment and the running down of its traditional heavy industries of ship-building, steel-making and mining, digs deep into its heritage for comfort.

Our walk is taken in countryside far removed from the pastoral beauties of Hampshire and Dorset, or the wild grandeur of Cumbria; and in the company of a man whose literary output is several worlds away from the fierce passions of Emily Brontë, or the descriptive eulogies of Francis Kilvert — though Kilvert would probably have been fascinated by him, and might have asked him for the words to some of his songs. The man is Tommy Armstrong, the 'Pitman Poet', and the location is the coal-bearing landscape north-east of Durham City where the villages run in straight rows of terraced houses up the sides and along the ridges of the gently rolling hills. They do not fit snugly in with their surroundings, as do

Weston Longville or Lyme Regis; they were laid out by the coal-owners on the surface of the land as quickly and cheaply as possible to house the families of the men and boys who spent most of their lives searching for the 'black diamond', and the short remainder wheezing in an armchair or workhouse. Now that most of the coalworkings are uneconomic, the pits are silent and the pit-heaps levelled into football pitches or weed-strewn waste ground. The pit villages, their *raison d'être* gone, are slowly losing the struggle to retain the separate identity and character of which they were once so proud; while the young men go to the Job Centres and dole queues of Newcastle and Sunderland, or sit around on their doorsteps with their fathers and grandfathers, hearing yet more tales of the life 'doon th' pit' that they themselves will never know. Stanley, the little town at the centre of this area, was as notorious a hundred years ago for Saturday-night riots and violence as any Wild West township, as the miners came roaring in with their pay packets and their enormous thirsts. The enormous thirsts remain — in Stanley I saw three generations of the same family falling off the same seat together after a session 'on th' beor' — but the pay packets have vanished with the coal. There is real bitterness and depression here where Britain's wealth was mined for so long; though even when the pits were in full swing, times were very hard. Few ex-miners have romantic memories of the pits or of the bosses; strikes, lock-outs, poverty and terrible pit disasters were harsh realities to men still living here today. What has been sapped is their pride — pride in their work, in their strength and drinking capacities, in their close-knit communities. The songs of men such as Tommy Armstrong help to keep the memories alive, and the humour, sometimes broad, sometimes black, that still flows naturally from the people of the area.

Little enough is known of Tommy Armstrong's life — his fame was purely local, and he lived and died unnoticed by the outside world. He was born at Shotley Bridge, County Durham on the 15th August 1848, and went down the pit as a young boy. He grew up a small, thin man, bandy-legged and with a great appetite for 'th' beor'. As he had fourteen children, extra income had to come from somewhere: so

Tommy sold his rhymes to travelling card-hawkers and broadsheet printers for a few pennies a time, and with his meagre pitman's wages just about managed to keep the wolf from the door. He moved around the area a good deal, living in the towns and villages and working their associated pits. Although he often refers in his songs to the experiences and feelings of the 'hewers' — the men who actually cut the coal at the face — there is some doubt as to whether such a frail man would have done this work, which demands the thews and sinews of the traditional sturdy collier lad.

Tommy knew the inside of Durham Jail — he was sent there for stealing a pair of stockings from West Stanley Co-op, a misdemeanour he tried to excuse to the magistrate on the grounds that they were the only pair of bow-legged pit socks he had ever seen, the way they were displayed in the shop, and must have been intended especially for him. He got a famous song out of the experience — 'Durham Gaol' — with its chorus which is still well known all over the North-East:

'There's nae good luck in Durham Gaol,
There's nae good luck at all —
What's the bread and skilly for
But just to make ye small?'

Tommy wrote hundreds of songs, a good number of which have passed into the area's folklore. The most celebrated is undoubtedly 'Wor Nanny's a Maisor', which tells the story of how Nanny and her man missed the train and passed the time until the next one at the pub. Nanny had 'nine glasses a gin . . . three gills a beer', was thrown out by the landlord, and went home in the paperman's cart. In fact, Tommy pinched the idea from another song enjoying success in the area at the time, 'Peggy's Trip to Sunderland' — local songwriters often borrowed each other's ideas and changed around the words to suit their own audiences. Unlike popular performers such as Geordie Ridley (famous for 'The Blaydon Races' and 'Cushie Butterfield'), Tommy only once tried his luck in the gold-mines that were the music halls of Newcastle and Sunderland. By all accounts he was not a very gifted singer or tune-smith, preferring to set his songs to well-known hits of the day and hear them sung by the local miners who best appreciated him. Unfortunately, Tommy was apt to lay about him with a stick in the pub if the company's performance of one of his songs displeased him; and he seems to have been rather too conscious of his great fame on his own patch.

After retiring from the pits, he continued to live in the area, occasionally writing letters in broad dialect to the local papers and adding a new song or set of verses for good measure. He died in Tantobie on 20th August 1920, at the age of seventy-two. The 'Pitman Poet' is well remembered in north-west Durham, whose life and times he chronicled with accuracy and humour for more than fifty years.

*　*　*

The walk begins at Beamish Open-Air Museum (212548), about two miles north-east of Stanley. Here you can spend a marvellous half-day before or after your excursion, wandering among working exhibits of north-eastern life and culture, past and present, including a fine transport collection and an operating coal-mine, put together painstakingly over the last few years and lovingly looked after and added to by the museum's enthusiastic staff.

Tommy Armstrong's trail starts as you face the splendid mansion at the heart of the Museum. Walk up the path on the right-hand side of the house, and cross a minor road into a gravelled lane to the hamlet of Coppy, a couple of hundred yards further up. Between a fir plantation and Peacock House on the left (212551), a narrow and overgrown lane leads downhill, over a wooden stile at the bottom, and along the edge of a field above a row of trees on your left. Where the trees end, keep straight ahead up the hillside to cross another stile at the top and continue along the top of the next field with the hedge on your right. The view is of rolling country, covered with pale, scrubby grass, evidence of the underlying coal. The terraced roofs and the spire of St Andrew's Church at Stanley stand on their hill-top away to the left.

Directly above the house called The Kennels, turn right at a green public footpath sign and cross a field to the narrow stile at the top. Just up the lane on the right is the Black Horse pub

(206554), a whitewashed little house which once served the settlement here known as Red Row, and which was the scene of the celebrated 'cutting contest' between Tommy Armstrong and a rival bard.

In 1886 or thereabouts, a Gateshead miner, William Maguire, came south to find work in the pits around Tanfield. Maguire fancied himself as a song-maker, and had soon set up in competition with the Pitman Poet himself. Tommy Armstrong, always touchy about his local fame, let it be known that he wasn't amused by this challenge to his crown; and after high words had been exchanged a meeting was arranged at the Red Row public house to settle the matter. Miners arrived in crowds from all over the area, some hoping to see the champion 'wipe the eye' of his opponent, others keen to witness Tommy being taken down a peg or two. The small rooms were packed with onlookers when the two rivals sat down opposite each other. The challenge was to improvise the best song from a theme chosen by the company.

The conventional suggestion of 'The Miner's Lamp' was turned down, as was one rather nearer to Tommy's heart, 'A Pint of Ale'. At last someone came up with a subject approved by everyone — the recent evictions that had taken place at Oakey's Pit near Stanley, where striking miners in the winter of 1885 had been put out onto the street from their colliery houses, together with their families and belongings. These men were still homeless and destitute at the time of the 'cutting contest', and the two contestants had a ready-made sympathetic audience at hand. Lots were drawn to decide who should present their offering first, and Armstrong and Maguire got to work, no doubt fuelled by a gallon or so of strong beer. Tommy Armstrong won the day by a landslide, and the hapless Maguire retired to lick his wounds in lifelong obscurity. His song followed him into oblivion, while Tommy's masterpiece, 'The Oakey Strike Evictions', remains one of his finest.

'It was in November and I never will forget,
The police and the candymen at Oakey's houses met.
Johnny the bellman he was there, squinting roond aboot,
And he placed three men at every house to turn the pitmen oot.

158

Chorus
Oh, what would I dae if I'd the power mesel'?
I would hang the twenty candymen, and Johnny that carries the
  bell.

There they went fre hoose to hoose to put things on the road,
But, mind, they didn't hurt theirselves with lifting heavy loads.
Some would carry the poker oot, the fender, or the rake,
And if they lifted two at once, it was a great mistake.

Some of these dandy candymen was dressed up like a clown,
Some had hats withoot a flipe, and some withoot a crown.
Some had nae laps upon their coats, but there was one chap
  warse —
Every time he had to stoop, it was a laughable farce!

There was one chap had nae sleeves nor buttons upon his coat,
Another had a bairn's hippin' lapped aroond his throat.
One chap wore a pair o' breeks that belonged to a boy —
One leg was a sort o' tweed, the t'other was corduroy.

Next there comes the maisters, I think they should think shyem,
Deprivin' wives and families of a comfortable hyem.
But when they shift fre where they live, I hope they'll gan to hell,
Along with the twenty candymen, and Johnny that carries the bell.'

[*bellman* = bailiff   *flipe* = brim   *a bairn's hippin'* = a baby's
nappy   *shyem* = shame   *hyem* = home]

The 'twenty candymen' got their nick-name from the
travelling sellers of candy, who would cry out 'Dandy-candy,
three sticks a penny!' around the streets of the pit villages. In
hard times these vagrants would turn their hands to the bailiffs'
bidding and act as the blunt instruments of the eviction orders.
They were universally hated, of course, and every boss's
bouncer was called 'candyman' in the area. In the end the
miners were powerless against the 'maisters' and their
candymen, and for the sake of their families usually (and with
a few notable exceptions) had to give in to the demand for
reduced wages. Tommy Armstrong's famous song 'The
Durham Lock-Out', about a strike caused by a demand for a
$13\frac{1}{2}$% reduction in wages, shows the spirit of the men at these
times:

'Let them stand or let them lie or do with them as they choose;
To give them thirteen-and-a-half we ever shall refuse.
They're always willing to receive, but not inclined to give;
Very soon they won't allow a working man to live.'

It also contains the splendidly vindictive verse:

'May every Durham colliery owner that is in the fault
Receive nine lashes with the rod, and then be rubbed with salt;
May his back be thick with boils, so that he may never sit,
And never burst until the wheels go round at every pit.'

Imagine the roar that went up as that verse was sung in a crowded miners' pub!

Opposite the Black Horse, turn left down the lane and left again up the road, which drops down into the valley of the Causey Burn, with a fine view ahead up to Stanley. In 300 yards at a left-hand bend in the road, turn right at a public footpath sign (205552) over a wooden fence into the field, and walk down to the quiet and well-wooded valley-bottom with the hedge on your left and Causey Hall Farm ahead on the far bank. Cross the burn by a footbridge and climb up the bank by concrete steps (known as the Devil's Steps) to go through the farmyard to the left of Causey Hall Farm, following public footpath signs. You cross the A6076, keeping straight ahead, and in a hundred yards turn right up the slope of a field (200551), keeping a fence on your right. From the brow of the hill you can look back to Red Row and the scene of the 'cutting contest'.

Along this path the miners of Tanfield came laughing and joking to the contest; and in a few more yards a view opens out across Tommy Armstrong's native land. To the left are the closely grouped houses of Tanfield Lea, at whose colliery Tommy worked for several years; ahead on the hill is Tantobie, where he died; and Tanfield itself, the pit village where he lived on and off for much of his life, is hidden away to the right by the trees along the Causey Burn. The foreground is dominated by the huge electric battery works to which the miners reluctantly turned as their pits closed and their traditional way of life came to an end. Beside the Causey Burn runs the now derelict Tanfield Wagonway, a monument to the

160

area's long association with coal-mining. As early as the seventeenth century coal was moved by horse-drawn wagons along a wooden wagonway from the Tanfield mines to the ships in the Tyne; and in 1727 the Causey Arch, the first stone railway arch ever constructed, was built across the burn just a mile north of the spot where you now stand. It is still there today, having been designated an Ancient Monument in 1935. In about 1840 iron rails were laid along the wagonway, and most of the wealth of the area passed along the line just behind the trees at the bottom of the valley. The wagonway survived until August 1962, when the southern section closed; and the remaining spur near Gateshead limped on until May 1964. The branch had been in continuous use for well over three hundred years.

Continue downhill by the fence, and cross the stile to reach the Tanfield Wagonway (195552). Turn left along the footpath now established on the line — right if you want to visit the Causey Arch (204560) — and walk towards Tanfield Lea. Soon you cross an iron girder bridge stamped '*Rayne & Burn 1848 Newcastle*'. Just beyond on the right was East Tanfield Colliery, served by sidings from the wagonway. Slag-heap and buildings have completely vanished.

At the road, turn left and cross the Causey Burn, which hereabouts becomes the Kyo Burn, then take the first gateway on the right and walk straight ahead across the field. In front of you is a vast area of waste ground, some of it converted into a playing field — the site of Oakey's Pit and Tommy Armstrong's strike evictions. Durham County Council are making a good job of clearing away and landscaping their derelict mines; the mountainous, smouldering slag-heaps where children and women clambered 'picking coals' have been levelled, and the winding gear and tall brick buildings dismantled. They have been replaced in many places by much needed playing space for children, or by new housing estates. Some local inhabitants, particularly ex-miners, have regretted their disappearance, feeling that such reminders of the county's heritage ought not to be wiped completely out of sight and out of mind.

When Tommy Armstrong was working at Oakey's Pit, a new overseer or 'keeker', Joseph 'Badun' Elliott, arrived from

Maiden Law, a few miles south of Stanley. One of the keeker's jobs was to keep count of the tubs of coal filled by each miner, and to reject tubs with too high a proportion of 'ramble' or loose stone among the coal. As the men were paid according to the number of tubs they filled, an over-zealous keeker could make himself very unpopular. 'Maiden Law Joe' made the mistake of crossing Tommy Armstrong, and found himself the subject of another of Tommy's satirical songs, 'Oakey's Keeker'. These five verses contain ample evidence of Tommy's devastating way with words:

Oakey's Keeker

Oh Oakey's, oh Oakey's, what makes you so bad?
It's enough for to make all your workmen go mad.
We should like very well to know what you mean,
The way you go on from the pit to the screen.
You treat us coal-hewers just as you think fit,
The wages are small that are paid in the pit;
But what we are making we don't really know,
Since they have sent us old Maiden Law Joe.

This famous old keeker must not understand
How we are tormented with ramble and band.
The ramble comes down, after firing a shot,
Among the loose coals, and it cannot be got.
By the light of a candle it cannot be found;
Daylight is different from being underground.
If this old keeker would only think so,
We would speak better of old Maiden Law Joe.

To do his duty is nothing but right,
But in hurting coal-hewers he takes a delight.
If he pleases the masters, that's all he cares for,
Suppose that he hungers poor men to the door.
At half-past six in the morning he starts
To fill up the box, which is only two quarts;
If he gets the first tub, how pleased he will go,
And say, 'That's a start for old Maiden Law Joe.'

He was at the Bank Foot — that's near to the Plain.
We only wish he was back there again.
While he was there he was doing the same —
He must have been born without feeling or shame.

They say there's a medium in every case;
He's not a fit man to have such a place,
For he has no feeling for men that's below,
This hairy-faced rascal, old Maiden Law Joe.

Now, Joey Badun, you silly old man,
You have done nearly all the ill that you can.
With age your whiskers are turning quite grey —
I think it is time you were starting to pray.
I never did like to wish anyone harm,
But I doubt you will go to a place where it's warm.
It's nothing but right to reap what you sow,
And they'll burn your whiskers, old Maiden Law Joe.

[*ramble and band* = loose shale that falls with the coal
laid out = disallowed
fill up the box = if there was enough loose stone among the coal in
a tub to fill the box, the keeker would disallow the tub, and the
hewer and his mates would not be paid for it.)

Maiden Law Joe was so mortified by this that he took
Tommy Armstrong to court over the song. However, when the
words were read out, the Bench could hardly keep their faces
straight, and with the Magistrate's observation, 'Well, you still
have your whiskers,' Tommy emerged from the conflict with
another victory under his belt. He did take things a bit far one
cold morning, when the keeker was warming himself by a
brazier; Tommy singed his enemy's whiskers by lobbing a stick
or two of dynamite into the fire!

The walk continues by skirting the new playing fields to the
left and passing under the Consett to Tyne Dock railway line
(193536), now falling into disuse since the great Consett
steelworks closed down. Carry on up the hill and cross over the
road at a left-hand bend (194533). Take the steep path that
runs up Watson's Bank to the right of Barn Hill; the central
hand-rail has been polished into shining brightness by
generations of Stanley palms. At the top you follow the road
round to the left and emerge at the bottom of Stanley's main
shopping street. Although the shops are modern and well
patronized, there are many tell-tale signs of economic
depression all round you – the decaying Pavilion Bingo Hall
next to St Andrew's Church Institute, the broken windows in

163

the old school just up the street, the high proportion of men in their twenties and thirties pushing prams and carrying shopping-bags for their wives. Stanley and Consett, the hard-core of the mining and steel-making industries in this part of the world, have been hardest hit by the recession of recent years. Their inhabitants are trying to make the best of a bad job, as they have always done; but nothing can disguise the stark fact that these towns are dying on their feet.

Continue on past the Church Institute and Bingo Hall to the new roundabout (197531), and take the A693 road, marked '*Beamish 2*'. After two hundred yards turn right at the King's Head pub down Slaidburn Road, with Stanley's Swimming and Turkish Baths on your left. At the bottom of the road, walk across a grassy field to a gap on the left between the bungalows of a new housing estate named 'Burns Close'. Ten yards further on is a little tree on the crest of the ridge, with a bench nearby (200527). Here is a good place to rest and admire the splendid view over fifteen miles of countryside. To the right, the towers of Durham Cathedral can be seen behind the trees in fine weather, while away to the left on the horizon are the smoking chimneys of Sunderland. Near at hand are the straight rows of pit villages on every hillside.

The little tree by your side, however, is of even more interest than the panorama, for it marks the spot where the great shafts of Burn's Pit once plunged into the depths of the earth. This quiet housing estate is built on the site of the slag-heap and buildings which on 16th February 1909 were the scene of one of the most terrible disasters in mining history.

'About a quarter to four o'clock on Tuesday afternoon an explosion occurred at West Stanley Colliery in north-west Durham. The whole of the back shift men and boys, numbering about 184, were down the pit at the time. . .
. . .The colliery, which is owned by Messrs Burn Brothers, is one of the oldest pits in the Stanley district. The men working at the bank were apprised of the disaster by flames shooting up one of the shafts, and by two loud reports, which were heard throughout Stanley, and quickly caused large crowds to assemble in the vicinity of the colliery.
. . .No fewer than 94 bodies had, up to ten on Thursday night, been recovered from the workings.

Messages of sympathy with the bereaved have been received
from the King and Queen, General Booth, and others.'
Newcastle Weekly Chronicle, 20th February 1909

In fact there were 201 men and boys below ground at the time
of the disaster. 168 of them lost their lives, some in the
explosion and fire, but most from the effects of the deadly
'after-damp' or choking, gas-laden fumes. Under the heading
'SURVIVORS' STORIES — Entombed Men's Terrible Trials', the
Newcastle Weekly Chronicle recorded instances of lucky
escapes and heroism, the most remarkable of which was that of
Matthew Elliott, aged twenty-nine. Another reporter on the
scene, from the *Newcastle Daily Journal*, marvelled:

'Matthew Elliott is said to owe his escape to a remarkable feat he
performed. He, in fact, climbed up the shaft from the Tilley Seam
to the Towneley Seam by means of a wire rope or "staple". He,
too, seemed to be in a very bad state, but can anyone wonder at
that, having regard to the experience he has passed through? The
distance between the two seams has been estimated at eleven
fathoms [nearly 70 feet].'

Above ground a huge crowd of rescuers, relations and
onlookers assembled.

'From miles around miners walked and cycled to the scene of the
disaster, and thousands flocked around the pit-head, discussing
eagerly, and with bated breath, the scanty details obtainable.
    For those who had relatives down the pit the suspense was
awful. Women, with only shawls around their heads and
shoulders, stood for hours anxiously awaiting news of their
beloved ones below. One poor woman . . . had no less than her
husband and four sons in the mine.
    The pithead is situated on an inclined waggon way, negotiating
which in the pitiless darkness was a matter of great difficulty to
those unacquainted with the locality. The immediate vicinity is
almost lampless, and the thousands of persons, whose forms were
silhouetted against the black skyline by the small gas jets
improvised at the colliery head, made an altogether weird and
depressing spectacle. There would be no sleep in West Stanley last
night.'
            Newcastle Daily Journal, Wednesday, February 17th 1909

A few photographs of the survivors accompany the report. One in the *Newcastle Weekly Chronicle* shows Robert Anderson of Hill Street standing at his door with his young daughter and his wife, her face still swollen with tears and her hands clasped painfully together in front of her white apron.

As the extent of the disaster became clear, Stanley was plunged into mourning. After the inquest on the bodies they were taken away in carts to their homes, followed by their families, to be laid out on the bed in the front room.

> 'It was then possible to form some estimate of the havoc that had been wrought in the town. All through the East End, the mining quarter, there were drawn blinds, and in almost every house there was affliction. In some particular streets there was only, perhaps, one house that had escaped the tragic consequences of the disaster. Kettledrum Street was an instance in point.'
>
> *Newcastle Weekly Chronicle*, 20th February 1909

Journalistic writing of the finest kind — descriptive, heart-touching and powerful — distinguishes these newspaper reports. They painted the grim picture superbly for a readership that relied entirely on the papers for news. Nowadays, familiar as we are with the aids given to the imagination by television pictures and radio sound-recordings, their style may seem overblown and in some cases patronizing, but they are marvellous examples of a type of journalism that was killed off by the modern news media.

Photographs of the funeral procession on Sunday show the streets of Stanley filled with sober, lined faces under bowlers and flat caps, as the long, long line of coffins winds under a leaden sky and drizzle to the churchyard, where the victims were buried in mass graves. The memorial recording their names can still be seen there.

Many old folk have been re-settled from the demolished terraces of Stanley in Burns Close and the other lines of new bungalows around the site of the disaster. If you take the time to stroll around and talk to the old men and women here, you can hear from actual witnesses the terrible story of those black winter days in 1909.

A modern footnote to the disaster belongs to Kevin Keegan,

the football star, whose grandfather performed heroic feats in rescuing 20 people from the pit, as well as one of the pit ponies.

From the bench by the memorial tree, take the path to the left of Burns Close that runs parallel with the A693 road. Turn right at Chaucer Close down Byron Close (no Armstrong Close — shame on you planners!) and pass Stanley Hall on your right, a wonderful house of nautical stained-glass windows built by a local scrap merchant, William 'Dinky' Bell. Turn left along the new road below Stanley Hall, and where it curves left follow the footpath through Ballater Close to the swing park at the end. Turn right here and make a bee-line for the spoil heaps of the open-cast mine ripping up the landscape dead ahead. The line of the 'inclined waggon way' which the *Newcastle Daily Journal* reporter found hard to negotiate now becomes clear — an embankment of rough earth and rosebay willowherb. At the foot of the 'rolley-way' (212578) turn up to your left along a narrow tarmacked path which leads to the A693 road, where you turn right and walk along with fine open views all around (but also cars and lorries!) to Co-operative Villas (219534), also known as 'Noplace'. A third of a mile beyond Co-operative Villas, turn left down a lane (219534), and immediately right down a track (218534) just before the fine Victorian Noplace School. Cross the busy new road and the high bridge over the Consett to Tyne Dock railway line. The route is now straightforward, a minor road which runs up to join the Beamish road above the Shepherd and Shepherdess pub. Tommy Armstrong would probably have turned right here to wet his whistle; you can follow in his footsteps if thirsty, or turn left to walk the remaining mile into Beamish Open-Air Museum.

The North of England Open Air Museum
Beamish Hall, Stanley, County Durham (Tel: Stanley (0207) 31811)
Includes: Visitor Centre, railway area, town area, colliery, Home Farm, exhibition in Beamish Hall.
The Museum welcomes research enquiries.

Murder, Moorland and Military Road with Dorothy L. Sayers

Five Red Herrings by Dorothy L. Sayers
First published by Victor Gollancz, 1931
New English Library paperback, 1968

(The Anwoth Hotel, Gatehouse-of-Fleet — Standing Stone Pool —
Ornockenoch — Gatehouse Station — The Pibble lead mine — Old
Military Road — Anwoth Old Kirk — The Anwoth Hotel. A varied
route of about seventeen miles by road, track, disused railway and
moorland. The walk can be shortened to about twelve miles — the
longer route is for determined walkers only, though most of it can be
driven round. The lack of formally marked footpaths on the section
between the old railway and the Old Military Road should not deter
you, as laws of trespass do not apply in Scotland as they do in England
— though landowners expect walkers to take reasonable care and to
follow the Country Code.)

O.S.– 1:50,000 Sheet No. 83 'Newton Stewart and Kirkcudbright'
1:25,000 Sheets No. NX 55 'Water of Fleet' and NX 56 'Big
Water of Fleet'

For our final walk we have come north of the Border, crossing
at Gretna Green that ancient boundary over which so much
blood has been spilled, and turning westward to explore
Scotland's unfrequented south-west corner that pokes out a
hammer-shaped elbow into the North Channel of the Irish
Sea. Far from the culture of Edinburgh and the industry of
Glasgow, this forgotten region abounds in small towns of grey
terraces and red sandstone public buildings, widely spaced
farmsteads and narrow lanes, and acres and acres of deserted
moorland and fells. The tourists that come here tend to be
those that have visited the area for years and enjoy the

Opposite: *Dorothy L. Sayers in 1930, by Sir John Gilroy*

unfashionable pleasures of market days, long walks, fishing expeditions and huge Scottish meals.

Passing through the narrow, dark-red streets of Dumfries and the isolated artists' haven of Kirkcudbright, you come to the little river-mouth town of Gatehouse-of-Fleet, a main street of grey shops and houses that runs from the town's War Memorial down to the bridge over the Water of Fleet. By the clock tower stands the Murray Arms, to which Rabbie Burns dashed to scribble down a song he had just composed during an evening walk — the Scottish battle hymn 'Scots wha' hae wi' Wallace bled'. Mud-spattered Land-Rovers are parked along the pavements, and in the pubs and shops the farmers rub shoulders with the local gentry whose fine houses are hidden in the woods that clothe the hills all round the town. Hundreds of thousands of acres are in the hands of a few landowners who have managed to preserve the town and its surrounding countryside in quiet and contented seclusion, affairs running on from year to year much as they have always done. The story of the feuds, blood-lettings and strategic marriages that moulded the situations of these few families would make a book in themselves — Murrays, McCullochs, Gordons and Cardonesses, names that still dominate the area.

Gatehouse itself has changed remarkably little since the 1920s, when Dorothy Leigh Sayers came to the Anwoth Hotel by the Fleet Bridge to gather local colour for the latest in her immensely successful series of detective thrillers featuring that slight but suave sleuth Lord Peter Wimsey. For several years she and her husband, Mac, had taken their holidays in nearby Kircudbright, where there was a flourishing band of artists who at one time had an exhibition running in Paris, and who met in each others' houses to while away the evenings in chaff and gossip. Dorothy L. Sayers, remembered locally for her loud voice, wide-brimmed hat and long cigarette-holder, was a complex and often forbidding person with a highly idiosyncratic character moulded by the isolation of her childhood and the uncompromising individuality of her outlook on life.

Born on 13th June 1893, the daughter of a clergyman, she grew up in out-of-the-way rectories in the East Anglian Fens, and made a name for herself at school and later at Somerville

College, Oxford, as a lonely and rather exhibitionistic young woman. She gained a First in French and after spells as a teacher, and a reader with the Oxford publisher Basil Blackwell, she joined Benson's advertising agency in 1922, and stayed there until 1931. By then she and Lord Peter Wimsey were famous, and thriller readers were thronging the bookshops to buy her latest offering, *Five Red Herrings*. Lord Peter survived through five more novels, the twelfth and last one, *Busman's Honeymoon*, appearing in 1937, after which Miss Sayers abandoned her money-spinner to write religious plays for festivals and for radio. Her twelve-part serialization of the life of Christ, *The Man Born To Be King*, attracted enormous interest, most of it favourable, when it was broadcast in 1941–2. Lecturing and broadcasting occupied the war years, and after the war she devoted herself to a three-part translation of Dante's *The Divine Comedy*, of which *Hell* came out in 1949 and *Purgatory* in 1955, to a stony reception from critics who felt she had outreached herself. She had not completed *Paradise* by the time she died on 17th December 1957, to the end an eccentric and cross-grained figure who enjoyed her fame but in spite of increasing loneliness greatly resented intrusions on her privacy. From her early years she had developed a sentimental obsession with religion. In middle life she turned away, but later her deeply intellectual involvement found expression in her many religious articles and plays.

Two events in her life cast dark shadows — her marriage in 1926 to Mac Fleming, a charming, weak and irresponsible ex-soldier whom she supported through drinking bouts and growing incapability until his death in 1950; and the birth in 1924 of her illegitimate son, whom she fostered with a spinster relation. She never named the father, and severed all emotional ties with the child, though she visited him regularly and supported him financially — another contradictory attitude in a woman who desperately needed to give and enjoy affection. She was a law unto herself, and still remains an enigma.

The plot of *Five Red Herrings* is so convoluted that any reader not a practised expert in detective fiction needs to read with a pencil and paper in hand to keep track of the characters and the constantly twisting and turning development of the story. In essence, it concerns the violent death of an obnoxious artist at Gatehouse-of-Fleet, and Lord Peter Wimsey's attempts to pick the murderer from a list of six suspects — the other five being the 'red herrings' of the title — each of them having a good reason for doing away with Campbell, an argumentative, drunken, lecherous ne'er-do-well. There are long passages of closely interlocking clues concerned with railway timetables, errant bicycles and forged tickets that make one's head spin, and the book is more of an intellectual exercise than an exciting read; in fact, it is not generally reckoned one of the better Wimsey novels.

However, its attraction as far as we are concerned lies in the detailed descriptions of the countryside and town of Gatehouse-of-Fleet — descriptions which still hold good today. The track of the murderer on his hugely elaborate alibi-establishing wanderings can be followed through the lovely and varied Galloway scenery, and other sites from the story visited *en route*. Unfortunately, the best traditions of detective stories have to be overturned and the identity of the murderer revealed before the walk starts, because of the references that are made to his activities along the way. So brace yourself, innocent reader . . . it was Ferguson, Campbell's neighbour, who did the dirty deed — although that statement itself hides a final knot which you will have to unravel by reading the book!

* * *

The walk starts outside the Anwoth Hotel, just beyond the lower end of the Fleet Bridge (597562). The potato scones mentioned by Miss Sayers in her foreword 'to my friend Joe Dignam, kindliest of landlords' are no longer served at the Anwoth, but the proprietors are still extremely kindly, and the place is still the choice of locals who prize a friendly and welcoming atmosphere.

You follow the tree-lined B796 road that runs in front of the hotel along the western bank of the Water of Fleet, passing Gatehouse School and climbing gently northwards in the

Gatehouse Station

verdant Fleet Valley. All around are the hard-edged outlines
of the hills which overlook the drystone walls that divide up the
cow pastures — Gatehouse is the scene of an international
'drystane dyking' competition every other year. The road itself
is unfrequented, its central white lines slowly fading as the soft
Galloway rains wash them away. Once it carried traffic to and
from Gatehouse's railway station, six miles away up the valley,
but since the railway's closure in 1965 few vehicles make the
journey up into the moorland wilderness.

After a mile you pass the turning on the left to Anwoth Old
Kirk. Go through the next gate on the right (592571) into a
field, and follow the wall down to a gap which leads to the
bluebell-carpeted banks of the Fleet. Directly ahead the river
makes a sharp loop to the east, its further bank a twenty-foot
high wall that encloses the dark, peat-stained Standing Stone

173

Pool (596573). This is a perfect spot for fishermen and artists, with the waters of the Fleet rippling round an island of willows and gorse that stands in the middle of the calm brown pool. Here Miss Sayers sited 'two little detached cottages side by side, looking over a deep pool'. In one of these cottages lived Campbell, the unpopular and hot-tempered artist, and in the other he met his death at the hands of his neighbour Ferguson. Herein lies the main mystery of the *Five Red Herrings*; for not only is there no trace today of the two cottages, their walls, sheds and gardens — but they never stood here at any time. Miss Sayers in her foreword confesses to having 'run up a few new houses here and there', and local speculation has identified the murder cottages as those still standing at Nether Rusko (585602) and at Woodfoot on the eastern bank of the Fleet (592595). Miss Sayers herself was silent on the matter, and the only certainty is that her imagination brought Campbell to his death in this bird-loud glade, where dippers and wagtails bob among the stones of the river.

The oak-lined banks of the Fleet can be followed through gaps and gates in the drystone walls as far as the Pulcree Burn (592576), across which are hung wooden gates to catch the debris of floods. There is no bridge over the burn, and you must return to the road just above Goatend Farm. The road up which Lord Peter Wimsey drove to interview the Gatehouse stationmaster winds into bluebell woods and emerges above the farmstead of Pulcree. From here it continues to climb up the long miles to the station — pity the erstwhile poor benighted traveller with bag in hand, sweating uphill for the late train to Dumfries! For a pleasanter and rather rougher route, take the lane on the left signposted '*Ornockenoch*' (587581) beside the low, whitewashed Pulcree Cottage, typical of most rural Galloway cottages. The track mounts by a drystone wall past pylons of extraordinary ugliness to Ornockenoch Reservoir, where real wildness marks the moorland surroundings. The two houses of Ornockenoch, one pink and one grey, stand among trees overlooking the reservoir, and the rough path climbs up a gully with a wall on the right, past a plantation of mixed conifers and broad-leaved trees to a marvellous view at the summit of the jagged Clints of

Opposite: *Standing Stone Pool*

Dromore ahead, backed by the huge hump of Cairnsmore of Fleet (2325 feet).

The track dips downhill to rejoin the B796 road below Upper Rusko. The Clints of Dromore, a harsh upthrust of rock from the upland plateau, begin to dominate the foreground, and to their right the spectacular Big Water of Fleet Viaduct comes steadily into view — 22 red stone arches that stride across the valley, bringing the old railway line from Castle Douglas away to the east through Gatehouse station and on westward to Stranraer and the Irish ferries. Opened in 1861 from Castle Douglas to Stranraer, and to Portpatrick the following year, the Portpatrick Railway was designed for the speedy transit of passengers and mail from Portpatrick (about forty miles west of Gatehouse) to Ireland, and the slower passage of cattle and other goods from Stranraer to the Emerald Isle. The whole operation was to prove a costly mistake, and Dr Beeching finally sliced off the moribund remains a century later in 1965. The grim grey stationmaster's house stares out across the bleak moorland beside the little-used Creetown to Dromore Road. You cross this road and keep, like Wimsey, 'straight on down a steep little approach, heavily masked by rhododendrons', which have now multiplied in wild splendour to take over the far platform. The neat, low station buildings are now a private house and the track between the platforms a marshy morass.

When Ferguson was carrying out his ingenious plan to cover up his involvement in the death of Campbell, he used the rhododendron-smothered platform of Gatehouse station to establish an alibi that would have been unshakeable but for Wimsey's unerring nose for skullduggery. Pretending to be on his way to an exhibition of paintings in Glasgow, Ferguson drove Campbell's car with its owner's body in the boot from Standing Stone Cottages up to the station. There he boarded the 9.08 to Glasgow, walked straight across the carriage, stepped out of the opposite door onto the track, climbed up onto the other platform, slipped out of the station buildings through the stationmaster's garden, and regained the road by way of the white-painted wooden gate at the top of the garden bank. Having established his journey to Glasgow in the minds of the station staff, he then drove the body to the Minnoch

Burn above Newton Stewart, dumped corpse and car there and took the bicycle which he had craftily brought on the back seat — having previously stolen it from the Anwoth Hotel — for a rather unusual ride to Girvan Station and another train for Glasgow. This one he really did catch, in order to be seen at the exhibition by a couple of artistic Kirkcudbright spinsters. Although the platform, buildings and even the garden gate are still there to be seen, it is rather hard to imagine Ferguson's trick actually working up here in the cold light of the Galloway moors.

Those who do not wish to do the full seventeen-mile walk can return to Gatehouse from here along the B796 road, passing on the way the two cottages with rival claims to Miss Sayers' murder site. At Nether Rusko, turn left down the lane with one claimant on your right (585602), cross the Fleet and turn right onto the minor road on the eastern bank. After half a mile you pass the second claimant on your right at Woodfoot (592595), and carry on past the golf course to reach Gatehouse main street just above the Murray Arms.

From the station the longer walk continues westwards for two miles along the old railway line. The ballast is still in place, growing thriving crops of violets in spring that quiver in the constant wind, and a more comfortable path can be found on the outside edge of the track-bed. The line runs as straight as a ruler between heathery slopes, combed into lines of drainage ditches, where curlews, blackcocks and grouse whirr and call among the small, shaggy black Galloway cattle. Half-way along on the right, an elaborate iron fence-post with an arrangement of cog wheels for tightening the wires stands on the bank, its weather-beaten lettering still decipherable — '*Francis Morton's Patent, Liverpool*'. Wind-whipped trees in a stony gully shelter the isolated farmstead of Craig.

You leave the old railway line at a handsome bridge, edged in rusty ironstone, and scramble up the cutting side to the road. Turn left for a few yards, then right onto the rough track (515616) that winds across the moor to the Pibble farmhouse. Before reaching the house, turn sharp left (517607) and take the old road to the disused Pibble lead, copper and silver mines, whose ruined engine house and banked-up reservoir lie under Pibble Hill. Just above the reservoir a faint track leads

177

The engine house, Pibble Mine

upwards across the hillside to the 'byngs' or spoil-heaps of the mine, and the entrance to one of the old levels (528605). A stream flows out of the mouth of the four-foot high delving, from whose cold black depths echoes the dripping of water in the flooded galleries beneath the hill-top. In 1862 this desolate spot was a bustling scene of industry, worked by the Champion Silver, Lead and Copper Mining Company, where miners hacked away all day underground, coughing their lungs out in the damp workings. The company collapsed after a few years' operation, as did the mine, though German prisoners of war worked it in a brief revival during the First World War. Now the rooks wheel around the arched window gaps of the ruined engine house, and cows graze in its shadow. Souvenirs of quartz stone, inlaid with green mineral stains, can be picked up here.

Two of the five 'red herrings' came here shortly after Campbell's death — Farren, one of the colony of local artists, who thought Campbell had been having an affair with his wife and was intending to throw himself down a mineshaft, and Strachan, the Gatehouse-of-Fleet golf-club secretary, who was looking for Farren to persuade him not to do Campbell a mischief. Miss Sayers has them both coming from Creetown, about four miles to the west, to the farm of Falbae (501615 — two miles from the Pibble Mine) and then taking a 'sort of shepherd's path' to the mining area. As with the exact siting of Standing Stone cottages, there is no clear-cut identification of the place, but Strachan reckoned it to be 'nearly two miles from Falbae', so it was probably here that the unfortunate secretary, chasing the drunk and distracted Farren in the dead of night, tripped up and fell down a forty-foot shaft. An old ventilation shaft for the mine still exists just beyond the fence above the entrance to the level, but it is unfenced, derelict and unsafe to approach. Strachan managed to heave himself out of the shaft after a desperate struggle, and made his way back to his car near Falbae. After tidying himself up he drove back to Gatehouse by a road which we will also take — and it must have been an extremely bumpy drive.

After pausing for a while to admire the marvellous view from the hillside over to Cairnsmore of Fleet and the Cree estuary, retrace your steps to the Pibble farmhouse (517604) with its superb walled garden of alpine plants. On the road just to the west of the house, bear left across boggy ground up to the angle of a stone wall with two gates equidistant from the corner of the wall. Climb over the right-hand of the two gates — in fact a double gate or stile — and then bear left up the hillside to another gate seen on the skyline. From this gate you walk down across a wide and lonely valley, crossing numerous small burns on the way, to the farm of Glenquicken (513594), backed by the TV relay masts on Cambret Hill. Join the track just below Glenquicken, and keeping to the right of the buildings climb up a walled lane to a gate. Turn right here, and carry on along a rutted track with a wall on your right to reach the Old Military Road from Creetown to Gatehouse (512585) just above Billy Diamond's Bridge.

Up until 1750 there were no properly surfaced roads in Galloway. It took the terrible shambles of troop movements during the '45 Rebellion to persuade the authorities that better communications were needed in this outpost of the kingdom, and the redcoats found themselves heaving stones, cutting, ditching and levelling all over Scotland. The road from Creetown to Gatehouse was carved out in 1763, and for twenty years was the only reliable means of communication in the area, until the coast road (said by Thomas Carlyle to be the finest drive in the realm) superseded it in 1785. Partly tarmacked, partly a rough lane, it switchbacks up and down for nine miles from deserted moorland heights to lush valley pastures.

The last six miles of the walk follow the Old Military Road, a straight slog with no direction-finding difficulties, but hard on the feet and the will. As you march out bravely in the footsteps of the redcoats, study the drystone walls that snake uphill on each side of the road. It is tempting to see in their construction the varied abilities of the road-building soldiers — runs of neat, well-sited stones of equal size, placed by a party of expert countrymen turned infantrymen, interspersed with the jumbled boulders and haphazard slabs shoved into line by an uncaring townee squad. In fact, the walls may have been built not by soldiers but by local farmers after the road was made — but imagination can be a great enlivener on these lonely homeward miles! Drystone walls being the characteristic features of this landscape, the Old Military Road makes a grand viewpoint from which to admire their enormous unbroken flow across the hillsides.

There are two remarkable views from the road — one just before the cattle-grid on the crest of Cambret Hill below the TV masts, looking back at the road wriggling its way past Knockeans Hill with the winding river Cree on the right, and a gleam of Wigtown Bay on the left; and the other a mile further on under Stronach Hill at a second cattle-grid, looking forward into the valley of the Skyre Burn where the road threads the plain under Kenlum Hill towards the sea in Fleet Bay.

The tarmacked road bends invitingly to the right at Glen Farm (548582), but the Old Military Road steers straight ahead as a stony track over the diminutive Glen Bridge, a shady nook with the Skyre Burn rustling over shallows among ash and willow trees. Glen Farm was once known as 'Slaights', and the road is known hereabouts as the 'Corse of Slakes' road — Corse being a road going uphill. Its other name is the

'Haugh of Anwoth' — Haugh being a road in a valley-bottom.
Along the bottom of the valley it runs, crossing the Kings
Laggan to Kirkbride road, becoming rougher and more boggy
at each step. It curves round St John's Well in a horseshoe of
mud and water among dense woodland, and emerges onto the
road opposite Anwoth Old Kirk (582562).

The roofless, crumbling old church building bears the
inscription '*Built 1627*' over the doorway, and the interior of
the red sandstone ruin is filled with old memorial tablets and
tombs. The largest, in the centre, carries verses on three of its
sides recording the virtues of three seventeenth-century local
ladies. One reads, in strong Scots accents, though doubtful
metre:

'Ze gaizers on this trophee of a tombe
Send out one grone for want of hir whois lyfe,
Twyse borne on earth and now is in earthis wombe,
Lived long a virgine, now a spotles wife.
Church keepis hir godlie life, this tombe hir corps,
And earth hir famous name.
Who then does lose — hir husband — no, since heaven
Hir saule does gaine.
Christen Makcaddam, Lady Cardynes.
Depairted 16 Iuny 1628. Aetatis Suae 33.'

Samuel Rutherford was 'called to the charge' here in 1627
before greater affairs claimed him — he went on to become
one of the founders of the Presbyterian Church, and a great
man in Scottish church history; though he left his heart in
Anwoth, as his verse declares:

'Oh, if one soul from Anwoth
Meet me at God's right hand,
My heaven will be two heavens
In Immanuel's land.'

In the 1820s the church was abandoned and a larger one built
nearby, but the ruins are lovingly cleaned and cared for in
honour of old Samuel and the other silent residents of the Old
Kirk.

For the final mile into Gatehouse, take the gated lane to the right of the Old Kirk and climb up through the wood to the Boreland Hills above, a folded series of grassy ridges that are overlooked by the obelisk put up to Rutherford's memory. There are no defined tracks up here, but continue straight ahead to drop down and meet the A75 coast road near the ruins of Cardoness Castle (591553), now a well-preserved monument open to the public, but in times past the scene of strife between the Gordon and McCulloch families. It was built in about 1468 by a McCulloch, appropriated by the Gordons and reclaimed by the McCullochs, before finally falling into Gordon hands again. In 1660 the last Gordon left it to the winds and rains.

On reaching the coast road, turn left and walk into Gatehouse-of-Fleet, sparing a final glance down to your right at the ruinous Port McAdam (595557), a derelict earthwork in the banks of the Fleet where a port once flourished briefly in the early nineteenth century before silting up and sinking its promoters' hopes in the slimy mud.

In Room 10 at the Anwoth Hotel, Dorothy L. Sayers wove the convoluted threads of the *Five Red Herrings*. In the cheerful bar downstairs I leave you, weary companion, at the end of the longest walk in this book — and the last.

The Dorothy L. Sayers Historical and Literary Society
c/o Roslyn House, Witham, Essex CM8 2AQ. (Tel: Witham (0376) 512025)
Founded in 1976 to 'promote the study of the life and works of Dorothy L. Sayers, to encourage the performance of her plays and the publication of books by and about her, to collect her other writings, and to propagate knowledge of this great scholar and her achievements'.
The Society publications include six bulletins a year. An annual convention is held.

Useful books
Such a Strange Lady by Janet Hitchman. Published in paperback by New English Library, 1976
D.L.S. Tour Guides published by the Dorothy L. Sayers Historical and Literary Society, 1981

Acknowledgements

Chief among the many pleasures of writing this book has been the contact I have had with so many helpful, patient and interested people — authors, museum curators, members of literary and historical societies, librarians, ramblers, local historians and enthusiasts. Without their cheerful willingness to be badgered and inconvenienced I could not possibly have put the book together.

I would particularly like to thank these people:

Tarka the Otter: Mrs Mary Heath of the Williamson Society; Ken Hunt, North Devon Area Librarian; Libby Lenton of the Vincent Wildlife Trust for information on otters; the Principal of Beam College, Torrington, for allowing me to look round the grounds; Miss Phyllis Morey of the Ramblers' Association (North Devon Walkers) for details of the route; John Adams of Torridge District Council for information on land ownership in the area; Pip and Denis Ives of Town Mills Hotel for hospitality, tall fishermen's tales and an early breakfast.

The French Lieutenant's Woman: John Fowles for his help and advice; Dr Joan Walker of the Lyme Regis Society.

Watership Down: Richard Adams for putting me straight on several blunders (and for a pint of Greene King IPA); Walter Long of the Basingstoke Ramblers' Club for his long and detailed letters of advice.

The Further Adventures of Doctor Syn: Coral Fowler, Hon. Secretary of the Dymchurch Day of Syn, who introduced me to Sexton Mipps, dragoons, sailors, smugglers (real and fictional) and the good Doctor himself; Miss Anne Roper of the Historical Association (S.E. Kent Branch), who generously allowed me to steal her valuable writing time; R.N.E. Dawe, Divisional Librarian at Folkestone Library; Daniel Thorndike, who corresponded with me about his father.

The Diary of a Country Parson: G. Bunting, Chairman (since retired) of the Parson Woodforde Society, who kindly invited me to the annual gathering at Weston Longville; all the members of that Society, who made an outsider welcome in their midst; Roy Winstanley, indefatigable editor of the Society's Journal, who brought the Parson vividly to life with his enthusiastic tales and explanations.

Tom Brown's Schooldays: Chris Lewis, master at Rugby School, who neatly caught the pass thrown at him by the Headmaster, and squelched round Tom Brown's Barby Run with me in a pelting rainstorm; the members of the Masters' Common Room for a superb dinner and good cheer; Mrs Jennifer Macrory, the Librarian at the school, who made books and documents available; Mr Brian Rees, the Headmaster, for allowing me free passage throughout his domain; F. Preece of the Rugby Local History Research Group; Fred Clapham, Secretary of the Rugby Group of the Ramblers' Association, for helpful advice.

Cider with Rosie: Laurie Lee, for marking my map with exact locations of places in his book, and for his kind interest; Alan Morley, Divisional Librarian at Stroud Library.

Kilvert's Diary: Mr and Mrs Morgan of the Kilvert Society, who gave up their time to pilot me round the Clyro countryside, and made many valuable suggestions; E.J.C. West, Hon. Secretary of the Society, for introducing me to them.

Wuthering Heights: Albert Preston, Hon. Administrator of the Brontë Parsonage Museum, who answered my queries comprehensively; Roy Richards, Chairman of the local branch of the Ramblers' Association, for his advice; Ian Dewhirst, Reference Librarian of the North-West Area Library, Keighley; Mr and Mrs Taylor of Ponden Hall, for bed, breakfast and a delicious pint of home-brewed beer.

Home at Grasmere: Messrs George Kirkby, Keith Moore and Jonathan Wordsworth, and the late Dr Peter Laver, all connected with the Wordsworth Heritage Centre at Dove

Cottage, for their generous help and advice; Hunter Davies for his suggestions (and for a copy of his excellent biography of Wm.).

Tommy Armstrong: John Gall of the Beamish Open-Air Museum; Tom Gilfellon (singer, cook, raconteur and slimmer), who fought manfully against temptation for most of a marvellous day's walking and talking.

Five Red Herrings: Ralph Clarke of the Dorothy L. Sayers Historical and Literary Society, for his enthusiastic help and advice; John Preston, Regional Librarian at the Ewart Library in Dumfries; Mrs Elizabeth Murray Usher for introducing me to many local landowners; W.J. McCulloch of Ardwall, who told me of his family's intricate and bloody history; and Liz Lyddiatt, who suggested this one.

I would like to thank the Henry Williamson Literary Estate for permission to quote from *Tarka the Otter*: and Laurie Lee and the Hogarth Press for permission to quote from *Cider with Rosie*.

For their kind permission to reproduce pictures, my grateful thanks are due to Fay Godwin (John Fowles); Richard Adams; Daniel Thorndike (Russell Thorndike); the Parson Woodforde Society (James Woodforde); Rugby School and Mr Reesby of the Geoffrey Creighton Studios (Thomas Hughes); Laurie Lee; the Kilvert Society (Francis Kilvert); Mr Richard Wordsworth and Mrs Mary Henderson (Dorothy Wordsworth); Beamish North of England Open-Air Museum (Tommy Armstrong); Dr Ralph Clarke of the Dorothy L. Sayers Historical and Literary Society (Sir John Gilroy's portrait of Dorothy L. Sayers).

I am especially grateful to members of the various literary societies associated with the writers whose landscape I walked. Some of these societies are world-famous, and enjoy a large membership and substantial funds — others are unknown outside their own tiny membership, and do their work unsung. All were fiercely devoted to their particular author, and happy to give unstintingly of their time and expert knowledge.

I would also like to thank Vivien Green and Richard Scott Simon for their help and encouragement; Marion Haberhauer for her quick and efficient typing; and Jane, who read and walked most of this book with me.

185

The author

The Maps

WALK 1

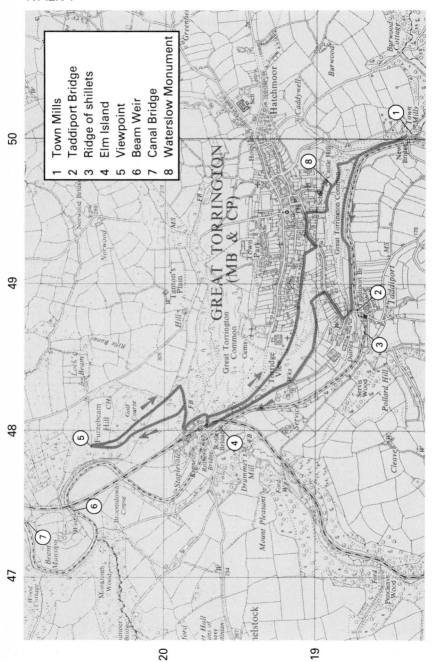

1 Town Mills
2 Taddiport Bridge
3 Ridge of shillets
4 Elm Island
5 Viewpoint
6 Beam Weir
7 Canal Bridge
8 Waterslow Monument

GREAT TORRINGTON (MB & CP)

1 The Cobb
2 Underhill Farm
3 Water pumping station
4 Goat Island

WALK 3

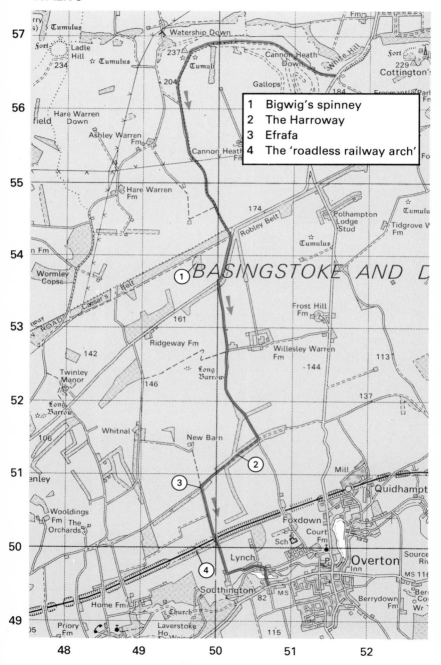

1 Bigwig's spinney
2 The Harroway
3 Efrafa
4 The 'roadless railway arch'

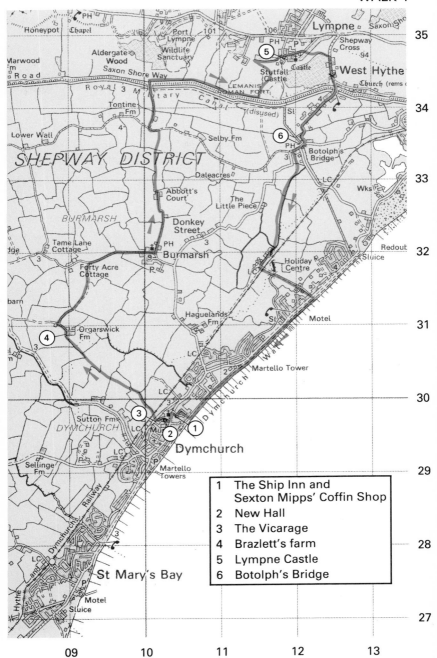

1	The Ship Inn and Sexton Mipps' Coffin Shop
2	New Hall
3	The Vicarage
4	Brazlett's farm
5	Lympne Castle
6	Botolph's Bridge

1   All Saints'
2   Weston Parsonage
3   St Margaret's, Lyng
4   Lyng Vicarage
5   Old Mill House
6   Lenwade Mill
7   Bridge Inn
8   Lenwade Bridge
9   Weston Old Hall
10 Weston House

07   08   09

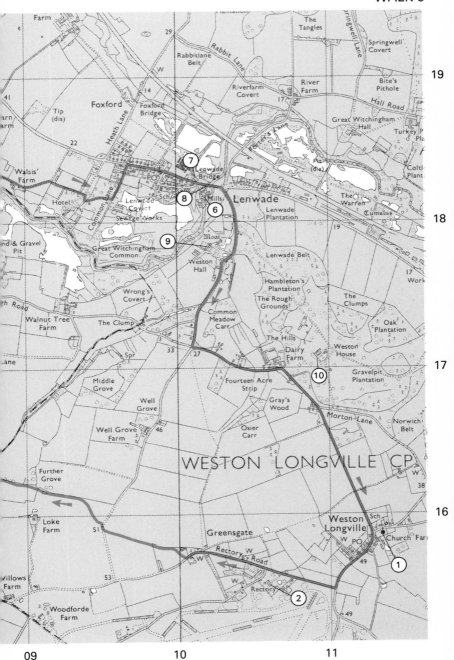

WALK 6

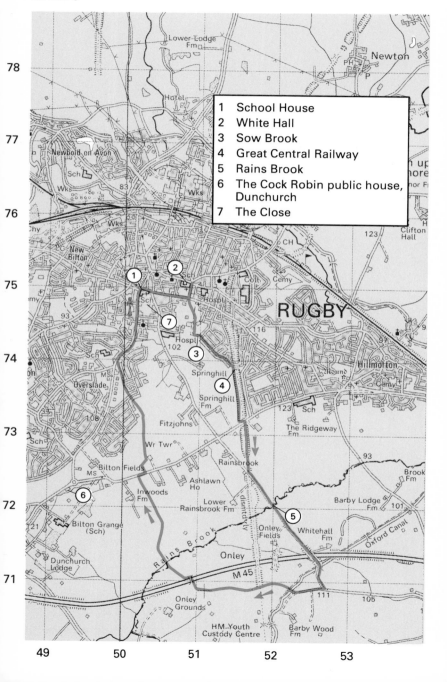

1 School House
2 White Hall
3 Sow Brook
4 Great Central Railway
5 Rains Brook
6 The Cock Robin public house, Dunchurch
7 The Close

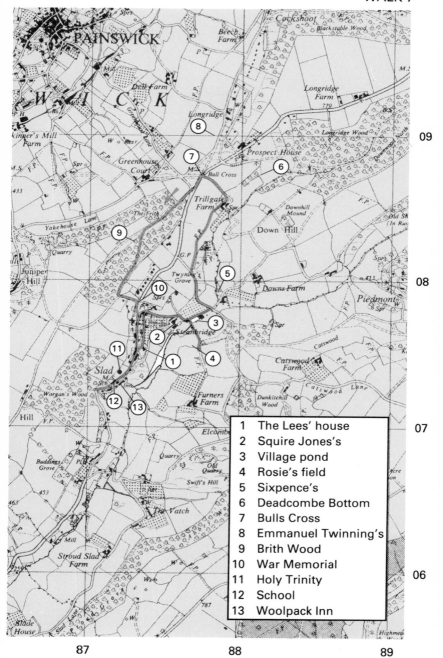

1 The Lees' house
2 Squire Jones's
3 Village pond
4 Rosie's field
5 Sixpence's
6 Deadcombe Bottom
7 Bulls Cross
8 Emmanuel Twinning's
9 Brith Wood
10 War Memorial
11 Holy Trinity
12 School
13 Woolpack Inn

WALK 8

1	Ashbrook House
2	Swan Inn
3	New House
4	Court Evan Gwynne
5	Birds Nest Lane
6	Little Wern-y-pentre
7	Gipsy Lizzie's
8	Pant-y-cae
9	Whitehall

10	Bettws Chapel
11	Hearts Ease
12	The Hom
13	The Cwm
14	Cwm-gwanon
15	White Ash
16	St Michael and All Angels'

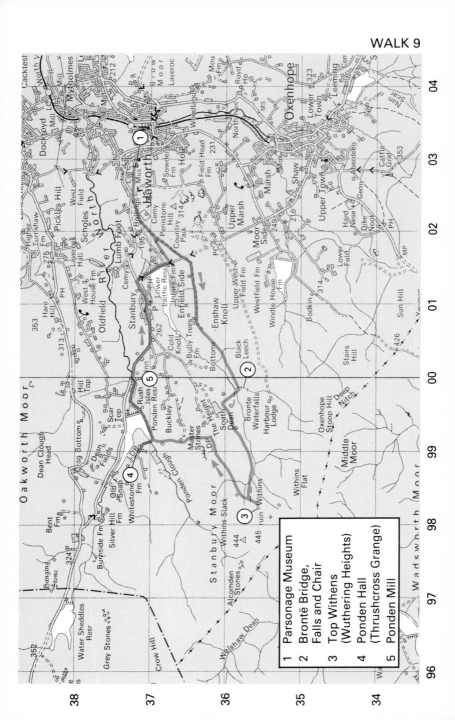

1 Parsonage Museum
2 Brontë Bridge, Falls and Chair
3 Top Withens (Wuthering Heights)
4 Ponden Hall (Thrushcross Grange)
5 Ponden Mill

WALK 10

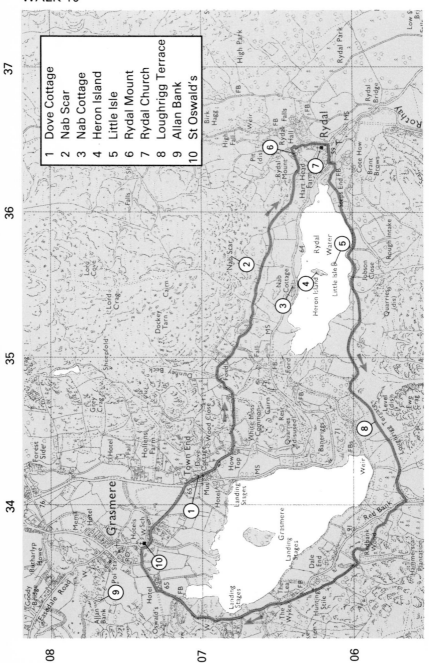

1 Dove Cottage
2 Nab Scar
3 Nab Cottage
4 Heron Island
5 Little Isle
6 Rydal Mount
7 Rydal Church
8 Loughrigg Terrace
9 Allan Bank
10 St Oswald's